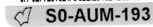

MY LORD SPEAKS

To
my father
and
my mother

MY LORD SPEAKS

Stephen Benko

JUDSON PRESS
Valley Forge

MY LORD SPEAKS

Copyright © 1970
Judson Press
Valley Forge, Pa. 19481

Standard Book No. 8170-0401-7
Library of Congress Catalog Card No. 68-20433

Printed in the U.S.A.

FOREWORD

Over a period of several years I was invited to lecture before various groups of ministers who came together to prepare themselves for the Lenten season. The purpose of these meetings was to discuss theological issues which would be helpful and stimulating for a successful Lenten ministry. My task at these meetings was to present an interpretation of the words of Jesus from the cross. These words are texts on which most preachers have delivered many sermons and from which they will have to preach again. I was requested to provide something different from the usual devotional meditations which people ordinarily hear at Good Friday services.

I tried to satisfy the need for new material on the seven words by calling attention to the historical background of the events surrounding Good Friday and the preaching values inherent in each word. Although these lectures were not meant for publication, the demand for them was so great that I decided to make them available in printed form. My good friend, Dr. John B. Rowland, the minister of the Wallingford Presbyterian Church, corrected the typed copy and gave valuable criticism. For the content I alone am responsible, and I wish to be the first to serve notice that much in this little book can be found in commentaries and treatises on the Gospels, that it lacks shockingly new and provocative statements, that it is not, nor was it ever meant to be, a strictly hermeneutical, exegetical, or philological study. Because of my primary interest in the historical background of primitive Christianity, the approach to these texts is more historical than anything else. Not even this consideration describes this book correctly, however, for it is designed to be a help to the minister who must preach and who will accept an historian's aid. This, and this alone, is what I claim as my original and honest contribution.

I hope that the nature of the book will make it welcome reading for all who are interested in the Christian religion in a positive way — not just as something to criticize. It is fashionable today to declare that the Christian church is finished, and that in order to be popular a religious book should try to outdo all others in saying things which contradict the tenets of traditional Christianity. But there are still millions who go to church, not because it is the "in" thing to do, but because it answers a need for them. They are the church. For them the words of Jesus are spirit and life, and the history of Good Friday has an existential meaning: It is the center of all history and the center of their lives. May such people find in this book more strength and a deeper understanding of their faith.

STEPHEN BENKO

Fresno State College
Fresno, California

CONTENTS

THE WORDS OF JESUS

Luke 23:34

"And Jesus said. . . ."

"O! but they say, the tongues of dying men
Enforce attention like deep harmony:
Where words are scarce, they are seldom spent in vain:
For they breathe truth that breathe their words in pain." [1]

Last words are often important words, for persons who know
that death is near usually do not speak unnecessarily or
foolishly. Speech is always a revelation because in speaking
we make public what is hidden in our hearts and minds.
How much more must this be true if words are spoken in
the conscious knowledge that one is communicating with the
world around him for the last time! Last words are usually
true words; confessions received from the lips of dying
persons often reveal secrets hidden for many years in the
innermost chambers of their souls. From words consciously
spoken as last words, we may get the clearest expression of
the nature and character of the man who spoke them. If
this assumption is true about the words of ordinary human
beings, how much more true it must be about the last words

[1] Shakespeare, *The Life and Death of King Richard II,* Act 2, Scene 1.

of Jesus, who with divine understanding faced his death on the cross.

"And Jesus said. . . ." Very frequently in the accounts of the life of Jesus we read this simple introduction to a saying of the Lord. Teaching and preaching were important aspects of his ministry, and he spoke many words. According to the Gospel of Luke, he was only twelve years old when he first took the Old Testament and explained it in the temple, and all who heard him were amazed at his understanding and his answers. How forceful were the sermons of Jesus! Remember the first sentence of the sermon with which he opened his ministry: "The time is fulfilled, and the kingdom of God is at hand; repent, and believe in the gospel" (Mark 1:15). Recall the beginning of the Sermon on the Mount: "Blessed are the poor in spirit, for theirs is the kingdom of heaven" (Matthew 5:3). Remember his beautiful parables about the flowers of the field, or about the wise and foolish men who built houses upon rock and upon sand. When we read these words of Jesus, we feel as the crowd did who listened to him and were astonished at his teachings, because "he taught them as one who had authority, and not as their scribes" (Matthew 7:29). Here in this sentence Matthew explained the secret of the power of Jesus' words: "he taught them as one who had authority." When we read the words of Jesus, we feel this authority behind them. None of us can remain indifferent to his words; we can either accept them or reject them, be overwhelmed or repelled by them, but we cannot ignore them.

It is interesting to observe in the Gospel narratives the different ways people reacted to the words of Jesus. The Pharisees were offended when they heard certain words (Matthew 15:12). When the rich young ruler came to Jesus asking him what he had to do to inherit eternal life and Jesus answered that he would have to give away his possessions, the Gospel describes the reaction of the young man with these words: "At that saying his countenance fell, and he went away sorrowful . . ." (Mark 10:22). Another time some people said of his preaching: ". . . he is mad; why listen to him?" (John 10:20). Again, when the scribes heard him, they were skeptical: "Why does this man speak thus? It is blasphemy!" (Mark 2:7). Because the words of Jesus were powerful words, the Pharisees tried many times to trap him in his speech by asking him questions which they hoped he would not be able to answer (Mark 12:13). But there were those who accepted the words of Jesus and believed in them. The fishermen caught nothing in the lake until Jesus told Peter to let down the nets. Peter answered, "Master, we toiled all night and took nothing! But at your word I will let down the nets" (Luke 5:5). "At your word," Peter said because he sensed the authority behind the words. When he finally realized that Jesus' authority was divine, this same Peter confessed, "Lord, to whom shall we go? You have the words of eternal life . . ." (John 6:68).

How great was the power in the words of Jesus! Matthew 8:16 relates that people brought to him many who were possessed by demons and that Jesus "cast out the spirits with a word. . . ." He healed a paralytic by telling him to be healed: "I say to you, rise, take up your pallet and go home" (Mark 2:11). When he saw the funeral procession of the young man from Nain, he said to the dead man: "Young man, I say to you, arise" (Luke 7:14), and the dead man arose! He said to the storm: ". . . 'Peace! Be still!' And the wind ceased . . ." (Mark 4:39). In a few cases tradition has preserved certain words with which he performed miracles in the original form as he actually spoke them in the Aramaic tongue. With the words *"Talitha cumi,"* he raised a little girl (Mark 5:41); with the word *"Ephphatha,"* he healed the deaf man (Mark 7:34). Power was in Jesus' words, super-human, divine power, irresistible authority, so that spirits and demons and even the elements obeyed him. Those who had the gift of faith were able to recognize this divine power and authority. Among them was a Roman centurion whose servant became ill and who asked Jesus to heal his servant. When Jesus agreed and wanted to come to his house, the centurion said, "Lord, I am not worthy to have you come under my roof; but only say the word, and my servant will be healed" (Matthew 8:8). Then he added one more sentence which beautifully illustrates how truly this Roman centurion understood the nature of Jesus: "For I am a man under authority, with soldiers under me; and I say to one, 'Go,' and he goes, and to another, 'Come,' and he comes, and to my slave, 'Do this,' and he does it" (Matthew 8:9). This centurion knew what authority was because he was under authority and he possessed authority. In the presence of Jesus he transferred what he knew about authority into the terms of the spiritual world. He understood at once that here was one whose authority was divine.

Yet, no matter how forceful a word may be, we still must realize that words in themselves carry no authority because authority lies within the person who speaks. Identical words might be spoken by two different persons, and the effect would be entirely different in each case. We could learn the words of Jesus and repeat *"Ephphatha"* or *"Talitha cumi,"* and nothing would happen. The miracle takes place because it is Jesus who says the word. When we read this sentence, "And Jesus said . . . ," it is equally important for us to consider both the words that are spoken and the fact that it is Jesus himself who speaks. The words of Jesus are effective only because he is the Son of God, the Messiah. As he himself explained to his disciples: ". . . The words that I say to you I do not speak on my own authority; but the Father who dwells in me does his works" (John 14:10). The words of Jesus receive their ultimate authority from the fact that in and through them God is working. Because of this we cannot by any means separate the words of Jesus from the history of Jesus, his birth, his life, his death, and his resurrection. The words he spoke and the works that followed (namely, that at his word the storm did cease, the paralytic man was healed, and the dead man did regain his life) together are the revelation of God by which he announced and established his new covenant. Let us understand well that Jesus did not merely speak about the new covenant of God, but he was that covenant; and he made it a reality with his death (Matthew 26:28). We cannot even say that Jesus preached the Word of God — indeed, a minister or a prophet can do that, but Jesus was more than a prophet or a preacher who proclaims a message. In the person of Jesus Christ, "the Word became flesh"; i.e., in the historical events of his life the message of God was proclaimed and his work was accomplished.

The event of the crucifixion itself, as it took place in space and time within the framework of human history, is a revelation of God. In this event God spoke to his creation announcing salvation. That Jesus found it necessary to utter certain words must be deemed a fact of utmost importance by all Christians, not only because the words are last words but because they are the words of Jesus Christ, the incarnate Word of God, who spoke and is still speaking out of a very special, indeed a unique, background. He speaks from the cross, and it becomes the place of reconciliation between God and men. He speaks in the hour of his death, and the cross is made the turning point of history and the center of time. He speaks at the end of the old age, and the kingdom of God draws near. We must keep these thoughts in mind when we read the simple account of Luke (23:33-34a), with which he introduces the first word of Jesus from the cross: "And when they came to the place which is called The Skull, there they crucified him, and the criminals, one on the right and one on the left. And Jesus said. . . ."

THE FIRST WORD

Luke 23:34

"And Jesus said, 'Father, forgive them, for they do not know what they are doing'" (author's translation).

"Father, forgive them, for they do not know what they are doing."

Πάτερ, ἄφες αὐτοῖς, οὐ γὰρ οἴδασιν τί ποιοῦσιν.

There is much disagreement as to whether or not Jesus actually spoke these words, for several important manuscripts omit this sentence. In such a case as this, there are two possibilities. If we assume that the sentence was actually an original part of Luke's version of the passion narrative, then some later editors must have omitted it for certain specific reasons. If we assume that the sentence was not originally in Luke's narrative, then other later editors added it.

In support of the first hypothesis, it may be argued that in the post-apostolic era, there was a strong tendency among the Gentile Christians to make the Jews responsible for the death of Jesus. The conviction grew among Christians that the destruction of Jerusalem was God's punishment upon the Jews for the crimes which they committed against Jesus. Consequently, Christians omitted this sentence because they were convinced that God had not forgiven the Jews for what they had done. It may be argued that the last words of the first Christian martyr, Stephen, as they are recorded in Acts 7:59-60, support this hypothesis. Stephen made two statements which are closely related to two sayings of Jesus from the cross, according to Luke. One saying of Stephen is: "Lord Jesus, receive my spirit." This parallels the saying of Jesus: "Father, into thy hands I commit my spirit!" The other saying of Stephen, "Lord, do not hold this sin against them," parallels this saying of Jesus: "Father, forgive them, for they do not know what they are doing" (author's trans.). Assuming now that the sayings of Stephen were based on the sayings of Jesus, one may conclude that this sentence was an original part of the Gospel of Luke and thus probably an authentic saying of Jesus.

As for the second hypothesis, the arguments generally run as follows: This saying shows a markedly "Christian" spirit and must therefore be a creation of the early Christian community. Or it was added by Luke himself, who was anxious to vindicate the Romans in the trial of Jesus, and with this sentence he tried to show that Jesus himself forgave his executioners and practically lifted the guilt from them.

This brief glance at the arguments for and against the authenticity of the saying shows us that neither of them is convincing. The problem cannot be decided on the basis of present evidence. Unless an older manuscript is discovered, we cannot do better than to accept the choice of the majority of the present manuscripts (among them the Codex Sinaiticus and many others) which do contain this saying. Thus, this word must be viewed as an authentic saying of Jesus Christ.

"Father, . . ."

Πάτερ, . . .

The Aramaic equivalent of this word is *abba,* which is derived from the noun *ab.* The meaning of *abba* is "my father," but the same form is sometimes used in the plural sense, meaning "our father." Jesus Christ probably said this sentence in Aramaic, and so the word he used here was "abba." This we may assert with reasonable certainty on the basis of Mark 14:36, where, in another prayer of Jesus, tradition has preserved for us the Aramaic address before its Greek translation: "Abba, Father, all things are possible to thee. . . ." It is, therefore, quite possible that whenever Jesus prayed to God with the words, "Father," "My Father," or even, "Our Father," he used the Aramaic *abba.* These words should be noted especially because at the time when Jesus lived, this expression was used almost exclusively in a secular and not in a religious sense. God was sometimes called a father of Israel and father of the individual Israelite, but the word "Father" was almost never used in place of the name of God. Only at the end of the first century A.D. did the use of the name "Father" become more frequent in the rabbinic literature in addressing God. Even then, in order to prevent any confusion with a physical father, the expression "who is in heaven" was added, which is exactly the form that Jesus used in the Lord's Prayer. Only from that time on was "Father" commonly used instead of the name of God. To the contemporaries of Jesus, this term was an intimate expression denoting the relationship of children to their physical fathers, an expression too intimate and irreverent to be used for God. Pious Jews must have been somewhat shocked when they heard Jesus addressing God this way, and they must have felt that Jesus blasphemously placed himself in a very close relationship with God.

In spite of Jewish usage, the primitive Christian congregations began to use this form in the liturgy, perhaps on the basis of the beginning of the Lord's Prayer.

On the lips of the Christians the word "Father" received a deep theological meaning, which was new and basically different from the later Jewish usage. The Christian understanding was that through the mediatorship of Jesus Christ a new relation between God and men was established, a relation which can be expressed by the word "sonship." God, the Father of Jesus Christ, is a Father to all who are "in Christ," and in this sense Paul wrote: ". . . you have received the spirit of sonship. When we cry, 'Abba! Father!' it is the Spirit himself bearing witness with our spirit that we are children of God . . ." (Romans 8:15-16; see also Galatians 4:5-6).

". . . forgive them. . . ."

. . . ἄφες αὐτοῖς . . . .

Forgiveness can be granted only when there has been sin. With these words of forgiveness Jesus thus characterizes his own crucifixion as an act which is under the judgment of God and, consequently, will have as its result either punishment or forgiveness. Jesus prays, ". . . forgive them. . . ." But who are "they"? Who is to carry the burden of guilt for the crucifixion? The Gospel does not say. The same mysterious simplicity permeates both this saying of Jesus and the whole description of the crucifixion itself. "And when they came to the place which is called The Skull, there they crucified him . . . ," says Luke. Where was Jesus crucified? At a place called The Skull. And where is this place? We are not told, and still today the exact location of the crucifixion is uncertain, except perhaps for the fact that it was outside the city walls. Who performed the actual act of crucifixion?

"They," says Luke simply. But who are "they"? The Romans? The Jews? Servants of the state or servants of the synagogue? We are not told this either. One may argue that the plural pronoun in verses 18, 20, 21, 23, 25, and 26 certainly refers to the Jews in general and that, therefore, the plural pronoun in verse 34 must refer to the Jews too. Yet it is certain that the plural in verse 33 ("they came to the place. . . .") does include the Romans, and we also know that a death sentence could be executed by the Roman authorities only. Also it is clear that the sentence "they cast lots to divide his garments" can refer to the Roman soldiers only.

An air of timelessness is in this part of the passion narrative. Where, by whom, and under what specific circumstances Jesus was crucified seems to be unimportant beside the overwhelming fact of the redemptive death of Jesus itself. The guilt cannot be fixed on any individual, or on any particular group of people, so that others can be vindicated. Jesus prays for sinners, and sin is a condition of the human race which cannot be limited to a certain time and a certain place, because it embraces past, present, and future generations; and no one is exempt from it. The perpetrators of the death of Jesus were not a group of Jewish noblemen or a group of Roman provincial officials, but the sinful human race, which embraces everyone. The death of Jesus thus became an event of such universal, all-embracing significance that very soon the primitive Christian community identified Jesus with the "suffering servant" of the Book of Isaiah, of whom it was said that "he poured out his soul to death, and was numbered with the transgressors;" that "he bore the sin of many, and made intercession for the transgressors" (Isaiah 53:12). The lapse of several centuries between the time of Isaiah and Jesus did not and does not trouble Christians. The condition of sinful humanity was the same in the biblical era as it is now. The need for just such a redemption as was accomplished by Jesus was realized then and is evident now. The cause for the death of Jesus was present then and is present now. Consequently, the redemption which was accomplished by Jesus has not only a retrospective but also a present and a forward-looking efficacy.

Forgiveness is the result of intercession. Here the atoning character of the death of Jesus is not considered as much as his office of Mediator, indeed, the only Mediator, between God and man. Jesus prays for sinners. This means that he intercedes for them with God. Between God and man now stands the Mediator Jesus, and access to God is now possible through him. This access is symbolized by the account of the rending of the curtain of the temple in the passion narratives. From a human point of view, the mediatorship of Jesus means that our needs and desires go to God through him; our prayers are cleansed and interpreted to God by him; and we appear before God through Jesus, as having gone through a purifying process which makes us worthy to be found in the presence of the Holy God. From the point of view of God, the mediatorship of Jesus means that God looks at us through Jesus and sees us as purified from sin. God deals with us through Jesus, in the father-and-son relationship, and accepts us all as his children.

Forgiveness is, therefore, always a redemptive act of God because it restores a relationship that was broken by sin. This redemptive act of God takes place in the events of Good Friday. On the cross Jesus Christ performs the act of reconciliation in a double manner: by deed in his capacity as Savior, insofar as he is laying down his own life as a substitutionary sacrifice; and by word in his capacity as Mediator, insofar as he intercedes for sinners. Thus, the new covenant is established. Sin, which barred man's way to God, is removed by the sovereign act of forgiveness; and the new communication between God and man begins through the mediating offices of Jesus Christ.

". . . for they do not know what they are doing."

... οὐ γὰρ οἴδασιν τί ποιοῦσιν.

The first word of Jesus Christ from the cross is a word of intercession asking for forgiveness. The coming of the new age is introduced by the act of forgiveness of sins, even as Jeremiah had prophesied:

"... no longer shall each man teach his neighbor and each his brother, saying, 'Know the Lord,' for they shall all know me, from the least of them to the greatest, says the Lord; for I will forgive their iniquity, and I will remember their sin no more" (Jeremiah 31:34).

Thus, the message of forgiveness was accepted by Luke and most beautifully expressed in the "Benedictus," which declares that God's messianic age will be brought about by giving:

"... knowledge of salvation to his people
in the forgiveness of their sins,
through the tender mercy of our God,
when the day shall dawn upon us from on high
to give light to those who sit in darkness
   and in the shadow of death,
to guide our feet into the way of peace."
                                    Luke 1:77-79

In both of these texts the idea of forgiveness is strongly connected with that of ignorance. The cause of separation between God and man, namely, the basic sin which must be forgiven, is man's ignorance of God and his will. This association of forgiveness and ignorance can be followed through both the Old and the New Testaments in texts such as Hosea 4:6, "My people are destroyed for lack of knowledge," and Luke 19:42-44:

"Would that even today you knew the things that make for peace! But now they are hid from your eyes. For the days shall come upon you, when your enemies will cast up a bank about you and surround you, and hem you in on every side . . . because you did not know the time of your visitation."

The intercession of Jesus is motivated by the presence of human ignorance, which is in agreement with Jeremiah's prophecy and the other texts which have been cited. Forgiveness is the power which drives away the darkness of ignorance and brings into full light the true nature and the saving will of God. This revelation is the basis of the new covenant.

The ignorance motif is particularly strong in the writings of Luke in Acts, as well as in the Gospel. In the Pentecostal sermon of Peter the crucifixion is attributed to ignorance: "And now, brethren, I know that you acted in ignorance, as did also your rulers" (Acts 3:17). And Paul says in the synagogue of Antioch in Pisidia: "For those who live in Jerusalem and their rulers, because they did not recognize him . . . fulfilled [prophecies] by condemning him" (Acts 13:27). It is questionable, of course, whether in these two cases, as also in the first word of Jesus, the term "ignorance" is used in a legal sense, such as the Latin would express by the term *per ignorantiam*. Actually, in the New Testament the word "ignorance" is used in two ways: one is the legal usage which expresses lack of information concerning a certain matter and an act due to the lack of information; and the other is the Jewish religious usage which denotes lack of knowledge of God. Which of these two meanings did Luke have in mind when he recorded Jesus' words in Luke 23:34 and wrote Acts 3:17 and 13:27? Although Luke, being a Gentile, may have been closer to the Roman rather than the Jewish usage of words, here he is quoting words of Jews — Jesus, Peter, and Paul — and it is inconceivable that any of these men would have used the term in other than the Jewish religious usage.

Furthermore, at least the two texts from Acts definitely refer to Jews; and if "ignorance" is a legal term, what was it that the Jews did not know? In the light of the ministry of Jesus, it cannot be said that they lacked sufficient information concerning Jesus and his claims. Thus, there remains no other alternative than that they were ignorant in a religious sense in not recognizing the redemptive work of God among them. This is clearly stated in Luke 19:42-44 and Acts 13:27, among other texts. In this same sense Paul used the word concerning Gentiles in his speech on the Areopagus: ". . . we ought not to think that the Deity is like gold, or silver, or stone, a representation by the art and imagination of man. The times of ignorance God overlooked . . ." (Acts 17:29-30). Here again, Paul thought as a Jew, using the word "ignorance" to designate the lack of knowledge of God. The same usage is found again in 1 Corinthians 15:34 and in Ephesians 4:18. There is no reason, therefore, why the first word of Jesus relating to ignorance could not be understood in this religious sense.

The ignorance motif in Luke's writings has been used for anti-Semitic purposes to put all blame for the crucifixion upon the Jews. Already the D Codex (Codex Bezae) had tried to emphasize the guilt of the Jews by sharpening the relevant passages. This tendency can be seen easily in Nestle's Greek New Testament, where the variants of Codex Bezae in the footnotes can be compared with the accepted text without difficulty. In Acts 3:17, where the text reads "you acted in ignorance," the Codex Bezae adds to this the word *poneron* reading: "you did EVIL in ignorance." Similar emphasis can be found in the other texts which deal with the idea of the ignorance of the Jews. The responsibility of the Jews, who provided the historical frame for the crucifixion, cannot be overlooked, but at the same time we must not lose sight of the universal character of the death of Jesus. If the Jews alone were responsible for his death, then the prayer of

Jesus would refer exclusively to them. If this is so, Jesus intercedes for Jews only — and salvation is limited to them. A sound exegesis of the text itself and the whole theology of a redemptive history contradict such a conception. No adequate understanding of the first word of Jesus can be achieved without putting it into the light of the all-embracing grace of God. No one has expressed this faith more beautifully than Paul in these words:

> "For there is no distinction; since all have sinned and fall short of the glory of God, they are justified by his grace as a gift, through the redemption which is in Christ Jesus, whom God put forward as an expiation by his blood, to be received by faith. This was to show God's righteousness, because in his divine forbearance he had passed over former sins; it was to prove at the present time that he himself is righteous and that he justifies him who has faith in Jesus" (Romans 3:22b-26).

THE SECOND WORD

Luke 23:39-43

"One of the evildoers who were hanged reviled him, [saying]: 'Are not you the Messiah? Save yourself and us!' But the other answered him seriously: 'Don't you fear God? You are under the same sentence, and we justly, because we receive [a punishment] worthy to what we have done. But this man has done nothing improper.' And he said: 'Jesus, remember me when you come into your kingdom.' And he answered to him: 'Truly, I say to you, today you will be with me in Paradise' " (author's translation).

"One of the evildoers who were hanged. . . ."

Εἶς δὲ τῶν κρεμασθέντων κακούργων. . . .

All of the Gospels report that Jesus Christ was executed along with two other men, his cross standing between the two others. Perhaps it was the intention of the Romans to have the "King of the Jews" surrounded by his "attendants" — a bad joke, which, if true, was probably aimed at the Jews to ridicule their political aspirations. According to Mishnaic traditions, the Jews themselves did not execute more than one person on the same day, but ample evidence from the works of Josephus and other sources indicates that this custom was not followed by the Romans. Moreover, Pilate, who came from his residence in Caesarea to Jerusalem for the high holidays, probably wanted to take care of as many legal matters as possible. Roman court proceedings started, as a rule, early in the morning. (This may be the reason why the Jews were in such a hurry to finish the proceedings before the Sanhedrin during the night.) We may conjecture that after the trial of Jesus was over, Pilate took up and disposed of other matters, the cases of the two men who were also condemned to die being among them. Death sentence was carried out immediately. These two, therefore, must have been sentenced shortly after Jesus.

What were the charges against these two? From the severity of the punishment we may conclude that the charges were of a political nature about which the Romans were especially sensitive. Luke calls the two men *kakourgoi*, i.e., "evildoers." Since Luke seems to have sought to please the Romans as far as it was possible, we may also assume that he qualified the crime committed by the men with respect to the Romans. Hence, the crime, which was something that was "evil" in Roman eyes, was most likely a political one. Mark and Matthew use the word *lēstēs* (Mark 15:27; Matthew 27:38) which is translated "thief" in the KJV and "robber" in the RSV. These meanings are only partially correct, because the New Testament uses another word to describe the common thief or robber, namely, *kleptēs*. (See Matthew 6:19, ". . . where thieves break in and steal. . . ." Also see John 10:1, 8, 10.) But to steal *(kleptein)* was not a capital crime and certainly did not draw the death penalty.

A *lēstēs* was more than just a simple thief or robber: He was a member of the so-called zealot movement, which was a political organization dedicated to the liberation of the Jews through an active, armed fight against all oppressors, especially, of course, the Romans. The zealots resorted to guerilla warfare because they were outnumbered by their enemies. In order to stay alive, they often took whatever they could lay their hands on; hence, the name "robber" *(lēstēs)* was attached to them.[1]

[1] Karl Heinrich Rengstorf, in Gerhard Kittel, ed., *Theological Dictionary of the New Testament*, Geoffrey W. Bromiley, trans. and ed. (Grand Rapids, Mich.: Wm. B. Eerdmans Publishing Co., 1968), vol. 4, pp. 257-262.

In their theology the zealots represented a messianic movement. They accepted no other form of government for the Jews except that of the "kingdom of God," for the realization of which they were ready to make the greatest sacrifices. Josephus referred to the zealots constantly with the word *lēstēs* so that this Greek word was even transliterated into Hebrew and used by rabbinic Judaism for the description of the zealot movement. The primary meaning of *lēstēs* is "robber, highwayman, bandit."[2] This usage is also found in the New Testament, e.g., Matthew 21:13, and 2 Corinthians 11:26. Jesus Christ used the word in Matthew 26:55: "Have you come out as against a *lēstēs,* with swords and clubs [as soldiers would] to capture me?" In this context the political meaning cannot be misunderstood. Or, when we compare the reference to Barabbas in Luke 23:19 (Mark 15:7), ". . . a man who had been thrown into prison for an insurrection started in the city . . . ," to the reference in John 18:40, "Now Barabbas was a *lēstēs,*" then again we must come to the conclusion that "insurrectionist" in Luke and Mark covers the same idea as *lēstēs* in the Fourth Gospel. Therefore, this word must mean a member of the zealot movement, not simply a thief or robber.

When Matthew 27:16 makes the remark that Barabbas was a notorious prisoner, then this may mean that he was an outstanding or well-known member of the zealot movement, maybe even a leader. Some manuscripts give the name of Barabbas as "Jesus Barabbas," so that, in this case, Pilate's question may have had a sarcastic undertone: "Whom do you want me to release for you, [Jesus] Barabbas, or Jesus who is called Christ?" (Matthew 27:17). As far as Pilate was concerned, both of them were political prisoners. Finally, he sentenced Jesus Christ on the basis of a political charge, and

[2] Walter A. Bauer, *A Greek-English Lexicon of the New Testament and Other Early Christian Literature,* William Arndt and F. Wilbur Gingrich, trans. (Chicago: The University of Chicago Press, 1957).

the inscription, "The King of the Jews," over his cross, may mean that he put Jesus in the same category as Barabbas, or the other zealots, only less dangerous because of Jesus' more idealistic conceptions about his future kingdom.

We may conclude, therefore, that the two men crucified with Jesus were zealots and that they were sentenced to death on this charge. In summary, the arguments in favor of this hypothesis are as follows: (1) the severity of the penalty; (2) in Mark and Matthew use of the word *lēstēs* for them, which was the common name for Jewish guerillas. Now that we know why these men were executed, we also understand why they talked to Jesus in exactly the way they did. They used messianic terminology exclusively. Even in the last minutes of their lives, they were interested in the matter which preoccupied their minds all the time. The first one asked Jesus if he was the Messiah, and the second one made a request concerning the future kingdom of God.

". . . *reviled him,* [*saying*]: '*Are not you the Messiah? Save yourself and us!*' "

. . . ἐβλασφήμει αὐτόν· Οὐχὶ σὺ εἶ ὁ Χριστός; σῶσον σεαυτὸν καὶ ἡμᾶς.

These words of the first man are essentially the same as the ones with which the rulers (meaning the chief priests, the scribes, and elders) mocked Jesus before: ". . . let him save himself, if he is the Messiah . . ." (Luke 23:35, author's trans.). According to Matthew 27:40, the other spectators also derided him in similar words, ". . . save yourself! If you are the Son of God. . . ." In addition to the rulers, who were the other spectators at the execution of Jesus?

Doubtless there were a number of the sort of people who would go to any execution, but there were probably many who were personally interested in this affair — secret sympathizers and perhaps even members of the zealot movement. They may have been the same zealot sympathizers who gave Jesus an all-out messianic welcome into Jerusalem on Palm Sunday, the most obvious form being delivered to us in the Marcan tradition: "Blessed is he who comes in the name of the Lord! Blessed is the kingdom of our father David that is coming!" (Mark 11:9-10a). These zealots had two reasons for coming to the execution: First, they wanted to be witnesses of the martyrdom of two of their own comrades. Second, they wanted to see Jesus die because he had so disappointed them. The mocking of the high priests and scribes was basically of a religious nature. They were scolding a blasphemer. (See Matthew 27:42-43.) The mocking by the passersby was motivated by political thoughts: They were reviling someone who did not live up to their expectations.

Any attempt now to analyze the mind of these people cannot be more than a conjecture. Yet we may try to understand the atmosphere that prevailed around the cross. The anger of the spectators may have been like that of a jilted lover, who, having given his best to the object of his love, has been most cruelly betrayed by the one in whom he had placed his greatest hope. These Jews in their anger felt that they had been humiliated by him whom they had acclaimed a few days before. Now he was dying the death of an accursed one. Were they shouting to give expression to their frustration or to express their hope that there might be a last-minute vindication for them? Perhaps everything was not lost; perhaps they were not fools at all, and another act in this drama was yet to come! Perhaps he was the Messiah and would reveal himself in a mighty, final act! "Save yourself, save yourself, and do show that you ARE the Christ!" The atmosphere was so charged around the cross that no one would have been really surprised if Jesus had come down from the cross and had declared the establishment of a messianic kingdom. This may have been what the Jews secretly hoped for; and, as the minutes passed, they cried more loudly and came close to the point where they would have broken down and wept: "Don't die, we need you! We want you to be the Christ; please, come down from the cross!"

One of the men crucified with him may have heard the people talking to Jesus in this way. He was not without some hope when he turned his head toward Jesus and asked: "Are not you the Messiah? Save yourself and us!" (author's trans.). These words are usually conceived as mocking Jesus, but I think we may be permitted to question this conception. Did that man really feel like jesting? And why would he mock Jesus? He had nothing more to lose, and what would he gain by ridiculing another man who was in the same condition? But hearing the words of the people, he realized with the instinct that is so highly developed in a guerilla that here was a chance of escape! Maybe he had not heard before that Jesus claimed to be the Son of God; maybe he thought that someone else, one of his own leaders perhaps, would take the title "Messiah." But the situation was desperate, and the man knew that only a miracle could save his life. Then he heard the people calling Jesus a Messiah, and suddenly all the hopes and expectations for which he had fought came back into his mind, and he thought: "Well, maybe, he IS a Messiah! Anyway, it cannot hurt me to ask him!" A little hope flared up in his soul, and he challenged Jesus to action. Doubtless he was concerned with one thing only, his earthly life. If Jesus could help him to escape death, which was so close now, that was fine. If he could not, well, then, nothing had been lost. The chance was worth taking, and he took it; for he was used to taking chances in life.

The Jews around the cross had something of this attitude themselves. The man's attitude toward Jesus was this: "You either give me some help in this situation, or we might as well forget about each other!" The Jews thought: "You either prove that you are the Messiah and do what a Messiah is supposed to do, or we don't want you. We are ready and willing to believe in you as the Son of God. We are prepared to crown you as the king of Israel; this you saw a few days ago. We are ready to follow you as our leader, but do what we expect from our leader, king, and Messiah. Start a revolution, drive out the Romans, restore our land! If you cannot, or if you don't want to do this, we are not interested in you, and we don't care what else you can do. Save yourself and us!"

Amid all this shouting, Jesus remained silent.

The silence of Jesus Christ

Both of the men who were crucified with Jesus talked to him. However, Jesus replied only to the second one and left the words of the first one without answer. This strange behavior of Jesus is described several times in the foregoing parts of the passion narratives of the Synoptic Gospels. At certain times Jesus completely refused to answer questions put before him, but at other times he willingly gave his answer. Consideration of these instances may shed some light on our present text.

The SILENCE of Jesus Christ is mentioned in the following situations:

Before the Sanhedrin: "And the high priest stood up in the midst, and asked Jesus, 'Have you no answer to make? What is it that these men testify against you?' But he was silent and made no answer" (Mark 14:60-61; Matthew 26:62-63).

Before Pilate: "And Pilate again asked him, 'Have you no answer to make? See how many charges they bring against you.' But Jesus made no further answer, so that Pilate wondered" (Mark 15:4-5). The parallel text is more emphatic: "But when he was accused by the chief priests and elders, he made no answer. Then Pilate said to him, 'Do you not hear how many things they testify against you?' But he gave him no answer, not even to a single charge; so that the governor wondered greatly" (Matthew 27:12-14).

Before Herod Antipas: "When Herod saw Jesus, he was very glad, for he had long desired to see him, because he had heard about him, and he was hoping to see some sign done by him. So he questioned him at some length; but he made no answer. The chief priests and the scribes stood by, vehemently accusing him" (Luke 23:8-10).

To these texts we may add the reports of the mocking by the soldiers in the praetorium (Mark 15:16-20), the mocking before the Sanhedrin (Luke 22:63-65), another mocking before Herod Antipas (Luke 23:11), and the mocking by the people on Golgotha (Mark 15:29-32). In all these instances, Jesus apparently ignored mockery as he did the remark of the first bandit.

The ANSWER of Jesus, according to the account of the Synoptic Gospels, was limited to questions put before him concerning his messianic claim. This happened during the whole trial only twice: once before the Sanhedrin, and the second time before Pilate. The texts are as follows: ". . . Again the high priest asked him, 'Are you the Christ, the Son of the Blessed?' And Jesus said, 'I am; and you will see the Son of man sitting at the right hand of Power, and coming with the clouds of heaven'" (Mark 14:61-62). Parallels are Matthew 26:63-64 and Luke 22:67-71. Pilate asked the following question, according to Mark 15:2, "Are you the King of the Jews?" And the answer of Jesus was, "You have said so." Parallels are Matthew 27:11 and Luke 23:3. Except in these two instances in which he affirmed his messianic claims, Jesus did not react in any way to any charge brought up against him, or to any question put to him. According to Luke, after these incidents Jesus speaks again (Luke 23:28-31), this time to those who are following him to the place of crucifixion, but the trial is over now.

The situation is different in the Fourth Gospel. Here Jesus enters into lengthy debates with both the high priest and Pilate, and it is recorded only once that he gave no answer: John 19:9. It is, nevertheless, important for us to know that the fact of the silence of Jesus was known to the author of the Fourth Gospel too, even though he made no use of it in the development of his theology.

What is behind the silence of Jesus? The high priest, who was apparently disturbed by it, suggested that Jesus had no answer to make (Mark 14:60-64; Matthew 26:62-65) because the charges brought up against him were true. But the Synoptics certainly do not suggest this. According to them, the charges were based on false testimony which Jesus could have easily refuted. Why, then, did the Synoptics point out so carefully this seemingly negative attitude of Jesus? Did they want to show that with his silence Jesus wished to demonstrate his contempt for the high priest, the governor, and the crowds? Some texts may support this hypothesis. We could understand that he did not want to get into any conversation with Herod Antipas, "that fox" (Luke 13:32), over whom he earlier passed such a sharp judgment. The point in Matthew 27:12 ("But when he was accused by the chief priests and elders, he made no answer") may be that it was the presence of his enemies, and the fact that the accusations came from them, that kept Jesus silent. That he did not react in any way to the mocking of the soldiers and the shouting of the people may very well be due to his sublime nature which refused to stoop to the level of the populace.

We may remember the contempt with which Polycarp treated the spectators in the arena who came to see his execution. The governor told Polycarp to convince the people concerning Christianity. Polycarp answered:

> I thought you worth reasoning with; for we have been taught to pay suitable honor to governments and authorities, appointed by God, if it does us no harm; but as for these others, I do not think they are worth my defending myself before them.[3]

Yet, we cannot seriously believe that contempt was the motivating force behind the actions of Jesus. He who came to fulfill the law would certainly show due respect to the high priest, even as Paul showed deference after realizing the identity of the person whom he had insulted. (See Acts 23:5.) Certainly, Jesus had no reason to show contempt for Pilate, who had tried to save his life. Contempt, therefore, cannot explain the silence of Jesus.

Possibly writers of the Synoptic Gospels wanted to point out that in the silent suffering of Jesus another prophecy of Isaiah had been fulfilled. They may have had in mind Isaiah 53:7, which states:

> "He was oppressed, and he was afflicted,
>   yet he opened not his mouth;
> like a lamb that is led to the slaughter,
>   and like a sheep that before its shearers is dumb,
>   so he opened not his mouth."

This hypothesis is much more probable than the previously suggested ones because we know that the figure of the "Suffering Servant" was already connected and identified with the person of Jesus in the earliest Christian tradition, and this very text probably inspired the author of the Fourth Gospel to call Jesus "the Lamb of God." Yet this prophecy does not completely fit Jesus because Jesus was not completely silent before his accusers. He did open his mouth when his messiah-

---

[3] "The Martyrdom of Polycarp," 10:2, in Edgar J. Goodspeed, *The Apostolic Fathers* (New York: Harper & Row, Publishers, Inc., 1950), p. 251.

ship was questioned; he talked on his way to the place of his execution; and he talked from the cross. The silence of Jesus must be explained in another way.

This explanation is to be found in the widely held idea that the absolutely ultimate Being of God, which cannot be further defined, is his Silence. Silence is not something that God does; it is God himself, which means that God is a *deus absconditus,* "The Silence that is broken by the Revealing Word" [4] to become a *deus revelatus* for the world. God reveals himself by his Word, and it is clear that the Word must proceed from Silence. "In the beginning was the Word, and the Word was with God, and the Word was God" (John 1:1). What the prologue to the Fourth Gospel expresses here in this sentence, the Synoptic Gospels express by pointing to his silence, which was the "exalted, sublime silence," not of the suffering servant of God only, but of God himself.[5] To know the real Jesus is to know him in his essential relation to God. This concept seems to be the message of the Synoptic Gospels, to present Jesus as he really is. Talking is a way of communication, but it is also a barrier. By being silent, Jesus compelled his adversaries to accept him as he was.

Thus, we understand that it was no accident that Jesus did answer the questions concerning his messiahship. The powerful "I am!" as recorded by Mark 14:62 involuntarily recalls Exodus 3:14-15, where God revealed himself to Moses with these words: 'I AM WHO I AM. . . . Say this to the people of Israel, 'I AM has sent me to you.' " Whether the author of Mark actually did have this text in mind can, of course, be

[4] Virginia Corwin, *St. Ignatius and Christianity in Antioch* (New Haven: Yale University Press, 1960), p. 123.

[5] Joseph Blinzler, *The Trial of Jesus* (Westminster, Md.: The Newman Press, 1959), p. 198. But Blinzler is quite right in pointing out that the Fourth Gospel also brings out "the sublime features in the personality of Jesus." During the whole passion narrative the Fourth Gospel pictures Jesus as having a "truly kingly dignity" (pp. 45-46). In this way the Fourth Gospel arrives essentially at the same result as the Synoptics do.

questioned, but undoubtedly in his answer to the question of the high priest, Jesus did claim to be the Son of God. This is the meaning of his answer to the request of the second criminal. Up to this point Jesus had been silent; he did not answer the mocking mob, nor did he answer the insolent suggestion of the first criminal. But Jesus opened his mouth and broke his silence when he heard the petition: ". . . remember me when you come into your kingdom." What did he say? "Today you will be with ME. . . ." A claim for divine authority cannot be expressed more clearly than this promise, and it definitely seems that the silence of Jesus Christ is emphasized by the Synoptic Gospels in order to provide a solid support for the words with which he affirmed his deity as the Son of God. Ignatius, the martyr bishop of Antioch, understood this clearly when he wrote in his letter to the Ephesians (15:1-2) :

> It is better to keep quiet and be real, than to chatter and be unreal. It is a good thing to teach if, that is, the teacher practices what he preaches. There was one such Teacher who "spoke and it was done"; and what he did in silence is worthy of the Father. He who has really grasped what Jesus said can appreciate his silence. Thus he will be perfect: his words will mean action, and his very silence will reveal his character.[6]

"But the other answered him seriously. . . ."

ἀποκριθεὶς δὲ ὁ ἕτερος ἐπιτιμῶν αὐτῷ ἔφη. . . .

Both the KJV and the RSV translations have *epitimōn* as "rebuked him," but the New English Bible has the words "the other answered him sharply. . . ." All these translations are grammatically possible because the verb *epitimaō* has all

---

[6] C. C. Richardson, *Early Christian Fathers* in *Library of Christian Classics* (Philadelphia: The Westminster Press, 1953), vol. 1, p. 92.

the following meanings: rebuke, reprove, censure, speak seriously, warn, and even punish.[7] I believe that the use of the term "speak seriously" is the best in this text because it points out the contrast between the insolent, disdainful behavior of the first man and the calm, more dignified reaction of the second. Also, in this story we see the two possible attitudes toward the messianic claim of Jesus: One can jest about it, as the priests and the soldiers did; or one can take it seriously, and the consequences will differ accordingly.

In contrast to the first man, this second one did not expect anything more from his life. He already had given up his life; nothing that life could offer him was interesting. He was a dying man, who had neither the energy to fight for his life nor the desire to live any longer. He knew that it was the last station on earth for him, and he did not try to escape. He looked back at his life, as if everything was past already, and confessed, "We are receiving the due reward of our deeds. . . ." This man realized the failure of his life, that his life and everything which he had done had collapsed. His hopes for the liberation of his country vanished, and he realized that all his hopes were based on false premises, on a false idea of the Messiah, on a phantom-Messiah who did not exist and could not come to rescue him and lead him to victory. Because he realized this, he was humble. He gazed at Jesus very seriously and spoke very softly. He was not in this world anymore. His hopes and his interest were already beyond life and death. He turned to the man at his side, who was called by the others the Son of God, and said: "Jesus, remember me when you come into your kingdom" (author's trans.) .

[7] Bauer, *op. cit.*

"Jesus, remember me when you come into your kingdom."

Ἰησοῦ, μνήσθητί μου ὅταν ἔλθῃς εἰς τὴν βασιλείαν σου.

The word "kingdom" must naturally be connected here with the idea of Jesus as "king." This identification was written over his head on the cross, and this was what the mockers called him. For Jewish ears this term must have sounded like a messianic (i.e., basically a religious) title, but political connotations were not entirely absent from its use. Therefore, the priests were able to turn a religious charge (blasphemy) against Jesus into a political one and present him before Pilate with these words, ". . . he says that he himself is Christ, a king!" (author's trans.) .

This title in itself could be understood by the members of the Sanhedrin as adding to the blasphemous claims of Jesus because from the earliest times in Israel, "king" was a special title of God. Thus, when Jesus answered affirmatively the question of Pilate, "Are you the king of the Jews?" he said essentially the same thing as when he answered affirmatively the question of the Sanhedrin, "Are you the Son of God?" Apart from the passion narratives, however, the word "king" *(basileus)* is very seldom used concerning Jesus in the Gospels, but the kingly title of "Lord" *(kurios)* is quite frequent.

The word *kurios* originally meant the owner of a possession, in contrast to the owner of a slave. However, very soon the meaning of the word took on religious connotations. In the oriental-mystic religions, gods were called by this name. In the emperor cult, the emperor was called *kurios.* At first, this title was used only in a secular sense, but later the term also conveyed a religious meaning attributing divinity to the emperor. Thus, a semi-official pledge of loyalty to the emperor developed. This pledge *(kurios kaisar)* played a very important role in the later persecution of the Christians because they refused to repeat the phrase. For them there was only one *kurios* — Jesus Christ.

The equivalent of *kurios* in Hebrew is *ādōn*. The Hebrew word originally meant "possessor, commander," but in a strict religious sense it designated God himself. The use of the word to denote deity has its roots in the Jewish liturgy where *Adonai* was substituted for the reading of the tetragrammaton YHWH. We cannot say that every time Jesus was called *kurios* in the Gospels his divinity is implied. Sometimes the meaning may be just a respectful way of address, as was the case when Pilate was addressed this way by the high priests: "Sir, we remember . . ." (Matthew 27:63). But there are many passages where we definitely have the impression that the word was used as a messianic title, e.g., in the Palm Sunday story (Mark 11:1-10) where the disciples borrowed the colt for Jesus with the words that "the *kurios* has need of it." Immediately afterward Jesus was greeted with these words: "Blessed is he who comes in the name of the *kurios!* Blessed is the *basileia* of our father David!" The use of the word only for a definite religious meaning developed after the resurrection and was accepted by the followers of Jesus as the final proof of his messiahship. The confession of Thomas *"ho kurios mou kai ho theos mou"* (John 20:28) reflects the belief of the primitive church in the kingly rule of Jesus both in the present and also in the eschatological aspect with respect to his coming again. Thus, a confession to the *kurios* Jesus became an essential part of the primitive Christian religious life (see Romans 10:9; Philippians 2:9-11; 1 Corinthians 12:3). According to the faith of the primitive Christian community, Jesus is *kurios kuriōn* (Revelation 17:14), and there is no other *kurios* besides him because nobody can claim the exalted position and authority that the resurrected Christ possesses.

In this light we must understand the idea of the kingdom of Jesus. When we approach the concept of the kingdom from the Old Testament idea of God as king, we naturally arrive at the idea of the "kingdom of God," but this form of expression never occurs in the Old Testament. The closest similar expressions are in the Book of Daniel (2:44; 4:3; 7:13-14), in which the kingdom of God means the restoration of the perfect kingly rule of God over the created universe. This concept is very closely associated with the messianic idea that the kingdom of God is an eschatological event, but the meaning remains indefinite as to whether the kingdom will be a perfectly restored earthly rule or a spiritual, heavenly rule. Although the universal character of the kingdom is strongly emphasized in the Old Testament, nationalistic expectations were never missing from Jewish thought about the kingdom of God. We see this very well in the zealot movement, in the Palm Sunday events, and even in the ascension account as found in Acts 1:6, where the disciples are still hopeful that Jesus (the *kurios*) will restore the kingdom *(basileia)* to Israel.

The message of Jesus Christ from the beginning was centered upon the proclamation of the kingdom. This word appears in the Gospels either as the kingdom of God, the kingdom of heaven (especially in Matthew) with reference to Jesus Christ, or just simply as the kingdom. But what did Jesus mean by the term — a present reality, or an eschatological hope? Is the kingdom to be identified with an earthly place and organization, or rather with a heavenly one? Without going into details, we may say that Jesus connected the idea of the kingdom of God with his own person and work. Thus, he did speak of the presence of the kingdom, but he also left the way open for an eschatological fulfillment. He definitely changed the emphasis from the material-political to the spiritual, and he presented the kingdom as the redeeming act of God, in contrast to any act of man. The redeeming act of God is manifested, of course, in the life, crucifixion, and resurrection of Jesus; and it is in these salvation-bringing events that the kingdom of God can be fully grasped. In the life, death, and resurrection of Jesus Christ, salvation did come, and the new age did break in; but the old age continues to exist until the final consummation. Between the death and the coming again of Christ, the world lives in two overlapping ages. Those who by faith accept salvation in Christ belong spiritually to the new age, although now they still live in the present age. But with the second coming of Christ, the existence of the present age will stop, and only the new age will continue to exist. It will be the complete realization of the kingdom of God. In this sense, therefore, it can be said that the kingdom of God is here and at the same time is coming, and that it is both a present and a future reality because the Son of Man is both here and coming. He gives salvation now and will bring it with himself.

Undoubtedly the man on the cross had an eschatological-messianic kingdom in mind when he asked to be remembered by Jesus. That he was promised "Paradise" instead does not make any difference because with this specific expression Jesus simply underlined the spiritual aspect of the kingdom as the heavenly abode of the redeemed ones. The man may not have possessed a clear theological definition of the messianic kingdom, but he certainly somehow realized the most important thing: that the door by which one enters into the messianic kingdom is Jesus Christ himself.

"Truly, I say to you, today you will be with me in Paradise."

Ἀμήν σοι λέγω, σήμερον μετ' ἐμοῦ ἔσῃ ἐν τῷ παραδείσῳ.

Although these words of Jesus are addressed to the second man on the cross, they also constitute an answer to the question of the first man, as well as to the Jewish mob standing around the cross. Jesus repeated, in effect, what he had already told Pontius Pilate in the praetorium, according to the account of the Fourth Gospel, that his kingdom was not of this world and that all those who expected him to fulfill their worldly desires were in error. He did not come to be king of a worldly kingdom; he did not want to be a revolutionary leader, and it was not his business to save anyone from execution. Jesus Christ came to open the way to salvation; thus, he offered to this man a place in Paradise. If anyone longs for forgiveness of his sins and for eternal life, Jesus will never deny this request. Therefore, the second man was with Jesus that very same day, but the first man and the Jews were not because they only wanted earthly life and what it could give them. They wanted to save their lives, and they lost them. But the second man was ready to lay down his life with Jesus, and so he found life again, stainless and glorious in the kingdom of God.

THE THIRD WORD

John 19:26-27

"Jesus, therefore, having seen the mother and the disciple whom he loved standing near, said to the mother: 'Woman, behold your son!' Then he said to the disciple: 'Behold, your mother!' And from that hour the disciple took her to his own [home]" (author's translation).

". . . the disciple whom he loved. . . ."

. . . Τὸν μαθητὴν . . . ὃν ἠγάπα. . . .

This passage is the second use in the Gospel of John of the phrase, "the disciple whom Jesus loved." In John 13:23 this disciple is described as leaning on the breast of Jesus or as "lying close to the breast of Jesus" so that Simon Peter asked him what Jesus was saying, the inference being that Peter was farther from Jesus and could not hear him well, while this disciple could. Twice this disciple is mentioned in the appendix to the Gospel of John (chap. 21), first in verse 7, where, again in contrast to Peter, he was the one who recognized Jesus standing on the beach, and again in verse 20 where he followed Peter and Jesus. At this point, after the question of Peter, Jesus spoke his cryptic sentence: "If it is my will that he remain until I come, what is that to you?" (v. 22a). The appendix makes an extra effort to emphasize that Jesus did not say that this disciple was not going to "die," only that he would "remain," and that it was not

Peter's concern. The tacit implication may be that when this disciple did die, this passage was intended as an explanation of his death. Or the whole section may have been intended to emphasize the fact that whatever the "beloved disciple" stands for will have a lasting role in the life of the church until the Parousia. In all these passages in John, the verb *agapan* is used, but in 20:2 in the account of Easter morning the verb *philein* occurs: "the other disciple, the one whom Jesus loved *(ephilei)*. . . ." Nothing can be deduced from the change of the verbs; but it is significant that in this passage also, the beloved disciple appeared to be in a race with Peter. They both ran toward the tomb and the "other disciple" outran Peter, but it was Peter who entered the tomb first (see vv. 5, 6, 8). Once before, in John 18:15-16, the mysterious figure of "another disciple" was mentioned but without the phrase that Jesus loved him. In spite of Bultmann's objections,[1] this disciple can be identified with the "beloved disciple" for two reasons: first, the expression "another disciple" is the same as in 20:2-10 which identifies the "other disciple" as the beloved one. Secondly, in 18:15-16 the difference between his position and that of Peter is clearly seen. Because the other disciple was known to the high priest, he was allowed to go into the courtyard while Peter had to stay outside. Then it was only at his intervention that Peter was admitted later. The thesis that the unnamed disciple in John 1:35-41 is also the "beloved disciple" is debatable.

Who is this disciple who was so favored by Jesus during his lifetime and was so distinguished by the word of Jesus from the cross? He is not identified by the author anywhere in the Gospel, and not even a personal name is given to him. Therefore, what do we know of him on the basis of the verses in which he is mentioned? We know that he was a disciple, but that does not even make him one of the Twelve,

[1] Rudolph K. Bultmann, *Das Evangelium des Johannes* (Gottingen: Vandenhoeck & Ruprecht, 1957), p. 369.

since the word *mathētēs* is used by the Evangelist for others also. He participated in the Lord's Supper, but the Fourth Evangelist never really says who and how many people were present at the Lord's Supper. Neither are the Synoptic Gospels unanimous in this matter. The oldest of the Synoptics, Mark's account, may very well be understood as suggesting that before Jesus arrived with the Twelve at the supper a number of disciples were already present preparing the meal (Mark 14:16-17).

We also know that the "beloved disciple" may have had a higher social or religious position, but this again could fit a number of people because we know that people of high social and religious standing were to be found among the followers of Jesus. He was present at the cross, but it is highly questionable that any of the disciples of Jesus would come or even be permitted by the authorities to come to the execution. Then, too, there is the report of Mark 14:50, which is referred to by John 16:32, that at the arrest of Jesus ". . . all forsook him and fled," including, of course, this "disciple." Finally, we may deduce from John 21 that the beloved disciple lived to an advanced age so that the rumor spread among the Christians that he would not die. Yet this idea, although popular, is nothing more than a conjecture since John 21 makes no reference to the age of the disciple. It is possible that this particular disciple was someone whom the others did not expect to die before the Parousia, but he did die. On the basis of this information, it is almost impossible to arrive at an historical image of the "beloved disciple." Among the followers of Jesus known to us in the Gospel narratives, he would possess the following characteristics: a man of means, a participant in the Lord's Supper, an influential citizen, one who stood at the cross, and one who was not expected to die. One might conclude that the "beloved disciple" was not historical at all.

Too many attempts have been made to identify the "beloved disciple" with an historical personality for us to enumerate them all. The best known and the traditional view is that he was John the author of the Gospel (see 21:24), who was also an eyewitness of all the events reported by him. Unfortunately, it is not easy to prove this, especially since, according to the witness of Papias, there were two men named John in Ephesus, one the apostle and the other a presbyter. It is difficult to determine which one of these was the eyewitness author of the Gospel. Even if we could, the problem of accepting 21:24 as an explanation of the foregoing verses would remain.[2] Others say that the "beloved disciple" is identical with John Mark (Acts 12:12), or with the apostle Paul (Galatians 2:20), the rich young man (Mark 10:21), or even Matthias of Acts 1:15-26.

Furthermore, there are other hypotheses concerning the "beloved disciple." The thesis was strongly advocated by F. V. Filson that the "beloved disciple" could have been Lazarus. Filson's main arguments are that Lazarus is the only one of whom the Gospel clearly says that Jesus loved him, that he lived close enough to Jerusalem to take Mary with him to Bethany after the crucifixion (see 19:26).[3] Perhaps the disciples thought that because he was raised by Jesus, he

[2] Papias says: "If, then, any one came, who had been a follower of the elders, I questioned him in regard to the words of the elders,—what Andrew or what Peter said, or what was said by Philip, or by Thomas, or by James, or by John, or by Matthew, or by any other of the disciples of the Lord, and what things Aristion and the presbyter John, the disciples of the Lord, say."

To this Eusebius adds: "It is worth while observing here that the name John is twice enumerated by him. . . . This shows that the statement of those is true, who say that there were two persons in Asia that bore the same name. . . ." Read the whole section in Eusebius, *Hist. Eccles.* III, 39, 1-8 in *The Nicene and Post Nicene Fathers,* Series 2 (New York: The Christian Literature Co., 1890), vol. 1, pp. 170ff.

[3] The Lazarus hypothesis is defended by F. V. Filson in his article, "Who Was the Beloved Disciple?" *Journal of Biblical Literature,* vol. 68, part 2 (June, 1949), pp. 83-88.

would not die until the Parousia. Then, when he did die (was the plan of the chief priests to kill him carried out?), perhaps he became the cause of a controversy among the disciples, which caused a need for an explanation concerning him in the appendix (see 21:23). These hypotheses show how wide the field is when one tries to identify the "beloved disciple."

The question of historicity could be solved with comparative ease if we possessed some record telling us with whom Mary lived after the crucifixion of Jesus. According to our text, it is supposed to have been the "beloved disciple." Do we have now any record that would indicate that Mary changed her place of residence and started to live in the house of John the disciple, or John the presbyter, or Lazarus, or any other of the followers of Jesus? The answer is no, we have no such record. On the contrary, Mary appears in Acts 1:14 after the resurrection in her old surroundings in the company of her other children, the brothers of Jesus. It is interesting to notice that this text in Acts refers to Mary in exactly the same manner and with the same sentence composition as was employed in the Gospel narratives: ". . . Mary the mother of Jesus, and his brothers." [4] This usage implies that no change had taken place in Mary's situation as a result of the events surrounding Jesus' death. With this statement we must come to the conclusion that the author of the Fourth Gospel meant something else by this incident at the cross than the recording of an historical event. In other words, the "beloved disciple" must be a symbolical and not an

---

[4] Matthew 13:55: "Is not his mother called Mary? And are not his brothers James and Joseph and Simon and Judas?" Mark 3:31: "And his mother and his brothers came"; v. 32: "Your mother and your brothers are outside . . ."; v. 33: "Who are my mother and my brothers?" See also Matthew 12:46-50 and Luke 8:19-21. Acts 1:14 uses exactly the same expression: ". . . together with the women and Mary the mother of Jesus, and with his brothers."

historical figure, and the understanding of our text must proceed from this hypothesis.[5]

"Woman. . . ."

Γύναι. . . .

The address "Woman!" sounds disrespectful and contemptuous to our ears. We would not address our mothers in this way. In the story of Cana, Jesus sharply rebuked his mother using the same word: "O woman, what have you to do with me?" (John 2:4). However, the rebuke of Mary is contained in the second part of the sentence ("What have you to do with me?") and not in the address itself. In itself *gunai* was quite a customary way of addressing a female person, and it may have been similar to our saying, "Lady!" or "Madam!" Jesus himself used this form several times, for example, "O woman, great is your faith!" (Matthew 15:28); or "Woman, you are freed from your infirmity" (Luke 13:12). Peter also addressed the maid of the high priest, "Woman, I do not know him" (Luke 22:57). Paul addressed the wives of unbelieving husbands, "Wife, how do you know whether you will save your husband?" (1 Corinthians 7:16).[6]

Because the word itself was not offensive, only the fact that Jesus does not call Mary his mother can be offensive to us. He could have said "Mother" *(Mēter)* both in this text and in the story of Cana, but he did not. As a matter of record, there is no text in the Gospels in which Jesus ad-

[5] The entire problem is well presented by Alv Kragerud, *Der Lieblings-junger im Johannesevangelium* (Hamburg: Osloer Universitatsverlag, 1959).

[6] We notice, of course, that *gune* in the New Testament may mean both woman and wife. For the whole problem, see article by Albrecht Oepke in Kittel, *Theological Dictionary . . .*, vol. 1, pp. 776ff.

dresses Mary as "Mother." Especially in this text where the word is coming from the cross, we could expect a more tender address than simply "Woman," because this word, in spite of all its polite and respectful character, does not contain the elements of a mother-son relationship. We must conclude that it was for this very reason that Jesus used this more formal address; he did not want to call Mary "Mother" in order to avoid any reference to a physical relationship.

"... behold your son! ... Behold your mother!"

... ἴδε ὁ υἱός σου ... ἴδε ἡ μήτηρ σου.

The traditional view is that with these words Jesus recommended Mary to the care of the "beloved disciple" and instructed Mary to consider this disciple as her son. For this reason, these words are often described as the words of love because they show the loving care of Jesus for his mother. Even in his last, painful hours Jesus took time to remember Mary and make some final, comforting arrangements for her. Why would Jesus do that? Roman Catholic exegetes usually answer that this text is a proof for their hypothesis that Mary had no other children besides Jesus. If she had had any, there would have been no need for Jesus to make these arrangements because his brothers and sisters naturally would have taken care of her. This exegesis is wrong. It is nothing but conjecture, which is not justified by the text. Furthermore, there is ample biblical evidence that Mary had several other children in addition to Jesus. But Jesus may have had good reason not to rely upon his brothers and sisters. During the lifetime of Jesus, especially during the last three years of his life while he was traveling about proclaiming the gospel of the kingdom of God, the relation between Jesus and his family was not good. The Fourth Gospel itself says, "... his brothers did not believe in him" (7:5) ; and there is good reason to believe that they considered him to be mentally unbalanced. One day a great crowd gathered around Jesus. "When his family heard of this, they set out to take charge of him; for people were saying that he was out of his mind" (Mark 3:21, NEB). Some translations read "friends"; but when we understand the literal translation of the words to be "those around him," meaning family or relatives, then we can understand Jesus' later refusal to see his family. He rebuffed them, asking: "Who are my mother and my brothers? . . . Whoever does the will of God is my brother, and sister, and mother" (Mark 3:33, 35).

It also appears that sometimes his brothers were trying to make fun of him. They accused him of seeking popularity. Not too long before his death they told him mockingly:

". . . 'Leave here and go to Judea, that your disciples may see the works you are doing. For no man works in secret if he seeks to be known openly. If you do these things, show yourself to the world' " (John 7:3-4).

The atmosphere between Jesus and the rest of his family must have been very unpleasant because of their unbelief. We have no reason to suppose, as Meyer suggests, that the future conversion of his family must have been known beforehand by Jesus.[7] Rather, because of no additional information, it appears that the family situation probably remained unchanged until after the resurrection. This alienation from his family suggests the reason why Jesus did not mention any of his brothers or sisters while on the cross and why he did not commend his mother to the care of his brothers. In addition, as there is no evidence which indicates that the brothers were present at the cross, of course Jesus

[7] H. A. W. Meyer, *The Gospel of John*, vol. 2, in *Critical and Exegetical Commentary on the New Testament* (Edinburgh: 1875), p. 351.

could not have talked to them at all if they were not there. Yet, this whole consideration is academic as far as historicity is concerned if, as has already been suggested, the Evangelist had a purpose in recording these words other than to report an historical event.

Let us turn briefly to Mary and see whether the relation between her and Jesus was such as would have moved Jesus to express a loving concern for her. It appears that the relation between Jesus and Mary was no better than the relation between him and his brothers. In those texts which so clearly show the estrangement between Jesus and his family, Mary is included, and she is always mentioned on the side of the brothers and never on the side of Jesus. There is absolutely nothing in the Gospel narratives that would give us the slightest hint of Mary's faith in the messianic mission of her son. There is nothing in these narratives that would indicate that the special revelations given to Mary, according to the Lucan accounts, influenced her attitude toward the activities of Jesus. Until after the resurrection she did not believe in Jesus, and Jesus knew this. Jesus' attitude toward Mary was determined by the recognition that the relation between them was simply a relation of the body. For Jesus the spiritual relationship with those who believed in him and accepted his mission was far more important. In this spiritual relationship Mary was not included, because she could not be counted among those who, in the words of Jesus, ". . . hear the word of God and do it" (Luke 8:21). "Who are my mother and my brothers?" asked Jesus; and then stretching out his hand toward, not Mary, but his disciples, he said, "Here are my mother and my brothers!" (Matthew 12:49). At the wedding at Cana, Jesus openly rebuked Mary. He was quick to reject the slightest attempt to suggest a closer relationship between himself and Mary. We are told in Luke 11:27-28 that after one of his speeches, ". . . a woman in the crowd raised her voice and said to him, 'Blessed is the womb that bore you, and the breasts that you sucked!' But he said, 'Blessed rather are those who hear the word of God and keep it!' " In the light of these incidents, we must seriously ask: Is it conceivable that after he declared so consistently and emphatically that the spiritual relationship was for him the primary concern, Jesus suddenly would change his mind and display such concern for Mary? Would not that mean an open admission that he was wrong in his former conviction and his attitude? Such a reversal certainly cannot be believed. But even if Jesus had wanted to show his concern for Mary, would he have done it this way? Would he have taken her out of her family circle and put her into an entirely new relationship? Jesus could not have been fulfilling the responsibility of the oldest son, because during the preceding three years he could not have been caring for Mary. The Gospel narratives clearly show that Mary was taken care of by her other children. They must have been willing to do the same afterwards, according to the situation presented by Acts 1:14.

Thus, it seems clear that the Evangelist wanted to do something more here than just describe an historical incident. But if it was not his purpose to write history, what is the meaning of these verses? The meaning is symbolical, and our task now is to find this meaning.

The Symbolic Meaning of John 19:26-27

Three persons are involed in this symbolical picture: JESUS, who is hanging on the cross and is about to die; MARY, his mother, who is taken out of her former circumstances and entrusted into the care and protection of someone strange to her; and finally, THE DISCIPLE, who has a very special relation to Jesus qualified by love, who is asked to give shelter to Mary. The Evangelist wishes to say something concerning each one of these three persons.

Jesus. What is actually taking place at the cross is a final dissolution of the mother-son relationship between Jesus and Mary. In this final hour, Jesus cuts himself loose from all material and earthly connections. The last of these connections is the one which existed between himself and Mary; i.e., that according to the flesh, she is his mother and he is her son. The mind of the Fourth Evangelist is working here in a theological way: Jesus Christ is eternally divine and is sent by God to the earth to fulfill a unique and special task. Mary was chosen as the human womb through which Jesus Christ appeared in the world as a human being. She was chosen for this sole purpose and nothing else, that through her Jesus Christ might receive a human body. Mary fulfilled this task, and then she was relieved from the excellence and burden of her motherhood of Jesus because his humanity is now coming to an end. The main characteristic by which Jesus is to be known is not that he is the son of Mary, a member of the human race, a link in the long chain of successive human generations, but rather that he is the eternal Son of God.[8] This breaking of the relationship with his mother is, therefore, a declaration of the divinity of Jesus Christ and just one step behind the open confession of

[8] The author of Hebrews was thinking on the same lines when he made a comparison between Jesus and Melchizedek, who is "without father or mother or genealogy, and has neither beginning of days nor end of life, but resembling the Son of God he continues a priest for ever" (Hebrews 7:3). It is possible that the Fourth Evangelist wanted to present the "Son of God" without father, mother, or genealogy. If the idea sounds too Gnostic to us, we must remember that this kind of Gnosticism is not strange to the Fourth Gospel. Also, let us remember that the gift of bread and wine (Genesis 14:18) which Melchizedek brought out to Abram offers an excellent point of connection with the theology of the Fourth Gospel, in which the sacramental elements of bread and wine have an unusually important role.

Thomas in the next chapter: "My Lord and my God!" (John 20:28).

Mary. In the Fourth Gospel, perhaps more strongly expressed than in the Synoptics, there is a definite emphasis upon the fact that the "old" which was in effect until Jesus came was replaced by the "new" which Jesus Christ brought. The old law was replaced by the new commandment, the old ritual by the new way of worship. It is interesting to notice that in the confrontation of the old and new, whenever Mary is mentioned in the Gospels, she is always among those representing the old, which is superseded by the new brought by Jesus. In the story of Cana, she represents the Jewish point of view, which does not grasp the real meaning of the specific miracle or the mission of Jesus and is, therefore, rebuked by Jesus. In the synoptic account of the incident when Jesus taught in the house and his mother and brothers came to see him, Mary is again the symbol of the synagogue and the brothers represent the Jews. They remained outside, but the new disciples, who were with Jesus within, represent the church, which Christ prefers to any carnal relationship. (See Mark 3:31, Matthew 12:46, and Luke 8:19. The antiquity of this symbolical exegesis of the Marian texts can be seen from the interesting fact that Tertullian in *De Carne Christi* 7, and Hilary of Poitiers in his commentary on Matthew 12:24 had already used it.) Here at the cross Mary not only represents the carnal side of the existence of Jesus — his connection with the human race and the Jewish nation from which Jesus cuts himself loose at this point — but she also represents the old covenant, the Jewish congregation. Jesus calls her attention to the fact that here at the cross is someone who is her son, and to whom she is the mother. She should recognize and lovingly accept this fact and willingly put herself under the care of the son.

The Disciple. The understanding of the figure of the

disciple comes naturally from the understanding of his counterpart under the cross, i.e., Mary. In the Gospels Mary
represents, generally speaking, the old (that is, the Jewish
point of view, the old covenant, the synagogue, the carnal
side of the existence of Jesus), and the disciple represents
the counterpart of all these, i.e., generally speaking, everything that became new by the coming of Jesus — a new point
of view, a new covenant, the Christian church, and particularly the spiritual aspect of it. Here, under the cross, the
disciple is reminded to recognize in Mary (and what she
stands for) his mother, and he is urged to take her into
his shelter. This word from the cross means that the Jewish
point of view should be absorbed by the Christian, the old
covenant by the new, the synagogue by the church, and a
carnal relationship to Christ be absorbed by a relationship
constituted by the Holy Spirit. Because the beloved disciple
so often is pictured as a competitor with Peter, it seems that
he should represent the opposite of that which Peter stands
for in the Gospel. Since in the Fourth Gospel Peter has an
outstanding role as the "shepherd" (21:15), i.e., the church
officer and administrator, then the beloved disciple represents
the spiritual aspect of the church. The emphasis in these
texts on the beloved disciple is on the importance of the Holy
Spirit as the constitutive power of the Christian church.[9] As
in so many other instances, Paul understood this important
point in the life of post-Easter Christianity better than anyone
else. He expressed it in a sentence that is as clear as it possibly
could be: ". . . even though we once regarded Christ from a
human point of view, we regard him thus no longer" (2 Corinthians 5:16). Let the Christian church never miss this
point: Jesus is no longer the earthly son of Mary, because he is
the risen and exalted Christ.[10]

[9] Kragerud, op. cit., pp. 26ff.

[10] For the problem of Mary in general, see Stephen Benko, *Protestants,*
Catholics, and Mary (Valley Forge: Judson Press, 1968).

THE FOURTH WORD

Matthew 27:46-49

"At about the ninth hour Jesus cried with
a loud voice: 'Eli, Eli, lama sabachthani?'
that is, 'My God, my God, why hast thou
forsaken me?' But some of those who
were standing by, having heard it, said
[to each other], 'This man is calling
Elijah.' And one of them at once ran and
took a sponge, filled it with sour wine,
and having put it on a reed, gave him
drink. But the others said, 'Wait, let us
see whether Elijah will come to save
him'" (author's translation).

". . . about the ninth hour. . . ."

περὶ δὲ τὴν ἐνάτην ὥραν. . . .

The Jews measured their days from sunset to sunset and divided them into halves, with night lasting from sunset until sunrise, and day from sunrise until sunset. Each of these half days was divided into twelve hours, regardless of the length of the daylight in summer or of darkness in winter. Thus, depending on the seasons, the hours were longer or shorter; and an equal division was possible only at the time of the equinox. At the equinox, six o'clock in the morning began the day, seven o'clock was the first hour, and so forth. The sixth hour was noon. The ninth hour was three o'clock in the afternoon, when, according to the account of the Synoptic Gospels, Jesus uttered his dying words. Thus, the time of the death of Jesus, which occurred at about 3 P.M., allowed just enough time for a quick burial, which had to take place before sunset, i.e., before 6 P.M. The time of the crucifixion itself is a controversial question because Mark

and John mention two different hours: Mark 15:25 says 9
A.M. (the third hour), and John 19:14 says that it was about
12 noon (the sixth hour) when Pilate delivered up Jesus to
be crucified. Matthew and Luke do not mention the hour
of the crucifixion, but they both, following Mark, say that
the darkness which fell upon the land started about noon
and lasted until about 3 P.M. Without going into a detailed
discussion of the discrepancy between Mark and John, let us
note that the hour of the crucifixion itself is accepted by most
theologians as having occurred around noon. Thus, we may
arrive at the following approximate chronology of Good
Friday:

In the morning: Trial before Pilate

Before noon: Sentence by Pilate

Around noon: Crucifixion; darkness over the land.

Around 3 P.M.:   The darkness lifted; Jesus cried: "Eli,
                  Eli. . . ."

After 3 P.M.:   Jesus cried again: "Father, into thy hands
                  I commit my spirit!" (Luke) ; "It is fin-
                  ished" (John). Immediately afterwards,
                  he died.

Before 6 P.M.:   Burial of Jesus completed.

"Eli, Eli, lama sabachthani?"
"My God, my God, why hast Thou forsaken me?"

The first half of this sentence is in Hebrew, and the second
half is in Aramaic; "Eli, Eli," is in Hebrew, and the rest is
Aramaic. The correct Hebrew text as it is found in Psalm
22:2 (22:1 in English versions) is as follows: *"Eli, Eli, lama
atzabtani. . . ."* The Aramaic translation of this, as it is
found in Mark 15:34, is as follows: *"Eloi, Eloi, lama sabach-*

thani. . . ." The simplest explanation of the discrepancy between Matthew and Mark is that Matthew, who used Mark, simply transformed "Eloi" into "Eli" and quoted the saying of Jesus this way. But now we have the Targum (the Aramaic translation of the Old Testament), in which the words of Psalm 22:2 are given back as follows: *"Eli, Eli, metul-ma sabachthani. . . ."* Except for the interrogative *("metul-ma"* or *"lama"),* the Targum's text is the same as the one quoted by Matthew. Which is the original of these versions? In which of these versions were the words actually spoken from the cross? The following possibilities are open: (1) Jesus spoke in Aramaic and translated Psalm 22 into his own words; (2) Jesus quoted the Targum; (3) Jesus quoted the Hebrew text, but during the period of the oral tradition his words were transformed into the common Aramaic and were later put down in writing in this way. While the first possibility would perhaps account for Mark's version, and the second possibility for the version of Matthew, the third possibility would account for both, because both of them would actually be based upon the original Hebrew text. This proposal is the most likely because Jesus, who knew Hebrew, would very probably quote a psalm in its original version and not in translation. And, finally, the Hebrew *"Eli"* could have been misunderstood for "Eli-jah" by the spectators, but the Aramaic form *"Eloi"* probably could not; thus, the Hebrew *"Eli"* explains the confusion of the crowd described in Matthew 27:47 and 49.

The whole problem has little significance except for the curious fact that the words were not translated into Greek along with the other words of Jesus when the Gospels received their present form. Of the seven words of Jesus spoken from the cross, this word is the only one which is quoted first in Hebrew-Aramaic; indeed, in the entire New Testament there are very few words which are quoted in the way Jesus actually uttered them, such as *"Talitha cumi"* in Mark 5:41, or

"Ephphatha" in Mark 7:34. Obviously, because the early Christian community attached great importance to these words, the attempt was made to preserve them in their original form. The important thing here is that these are the words of the Twenty-second Psalm. In his last hour Jesus recited this psalm, which is so full of important theological implications. Although tradition preserved only the first line of this psalm, Jesus very probably recited the whole psalm. The Gospel writers did not put it into the text because of its length and because they assumed that everyone knew the entire psalm. That the use of only the first verse was common practice among ancient Jewish writers must be kept in mind if we want to come to an understanding of this saying of Jesus.

The most common mistake committed concerning this word is to treat it independently of the rest of Psalm 22. It is assumed that Jesus said only this much and, therefore, meant only as much as is included in the sentence, "My God, my God, why hast thou forsaken me?" On this basis, then, the question must be raised whether or not Jesus was actually forsaken by God in the hour of his death. Answers to this question vary. The very idea that God forsook Jesus seems blasphemous to some people, and they try to prove that this could not have happened and did not happen. Others connect this word with the humanity of Jesus and answer that in this hour of anguish the spirit of Jesus sank to a low point, and he actually felt forsaken by God. Still others, considering the redemptive work of Jesus on the cross, believe in the soteriological necessity that he be forsaken by God. They reason that Jesus had to go through an experience of complete suffering and humiliation, including the greatest suffering and humiliation of all, that of being forsaken by God. Actually, all these arguments miss the point entirely. A similar distortion of meaning would occur if one would discuss the idea of silver mining on the basis of Job 28:1, "Surely, there is a mine for silver . . . ," whereas anyone who reads the whole chapter will easily understand that this first verse is merely the introduction to the development of a series of thoughts. The turning point comes only in verse 13 as the idea of the inaccessibility of wisdom to men crystallizes. In the case of the Twenty-second Psalm, we face a similar problem. If we cut off the first verse from the whole body of the psalm, we cannot understand the basic idea of the psalm, and we cannot understand what Jesus had in mind when he quoted this hymn.

The Twenty-second Psalm

The inscription of the Twenty-second Psalm, "According to the Hind of the Dawn," probably refers to the title or the beginning of another song, the tune to which this psalm was also sung. The psalm was probably used in the worship of the congregation as several references in it indicate, e.g., verse 22: ". . . in the midst of the congregation I will praise thee," or verse 25: "From thee comes my praise in the great congregation." It can be divided into two main parts: the first comprises verses 1-21 and deals with the complaints of the individual and his plea to God for help; the second includes verses 22-31 and contains a thanksgiving to God. Apart from this division, there is little order in the development of the psalm; the thoughts of the author wander freely; at one time they are concentrated on God, then on the adversaries, then again on the author. This pathetic wandering of thoughts impresses the reader as a dramatic and genuine search for fellowship with God.

The psalm starts with a desperate cry of a man whose whole existence depends on God, and who realizes the immense distance that separates him from the holy God. The psalmist knows no answer to the ancient question, "Why is God silent?" But he remembers at once that he is a member of that community which owes its national independence to a redeeming act of God. This knowledge gives him temporary comfort only; then he is overwhelmed again by the feeling of his lowliness and oppressed by his adversaries who mock him because of his reliance on God. In this condition, he can only confess the faith which has been his since his birth. Yet again he must come back to his miserable condition and to his enemies, whom he vividly describes. He does not see any other way for himself unless God acts on his behalf. With this prayer the first half of the psalm ends, and we see that even this "negative" part of it displays a deep faith which is so strong that it cannot be shaken even by the failure to find a hidden and silent God. Another feature which distinguishes this psalm from many others which deal with enemies and adversaries is the fact that there is no request for their punishment and the satisfaction of revenge.

The second part begins with a call of the psalmist to the congregation to praise God. The great distance between himself and God has been finally overcome, because God heard his cry. It was, therefore, not the psalmist who reestablished relationship with God, but it was God who stooped down to him and who, in spite of the miserable condition of the psalmist, ". . . has not despised or abhorred the affliction of the afflicted; and he has not hid his face from him . . ." (v. 24). The psalmist's joy is so great that he extends his call to "all sons of Israel" — which may include his former enemies and adversaries also. He plans to pay his vows in the presence of the whole congregation and invite the poor to a feast as an expression of his gratitude and joy. But the praise of God must not be limited to the nation of Israel only; all families of nations, the whole earth, must recognize God as Lord. "For dominion belongs to the Lord, and he rules over the nations" (v. 28). The kingdom of God is breaking in; there are no limits to it in either space or time. Not even death can hinder its coming, because even the dead will be included in it. Generation after generation will remember and proclaim the saving acts of God until his dominion extends over all.

Jesus must have seen in the Twenty-second Psalm many similarities between his suffering and that of the psalmist. Also, the theological implications of this psalm may have stimulated his mind while he was facing death on the cross.

Taking the psalm for the basis, the following similarities are noted:

Verse   7:   "All who see me mock at me,
                   they make mouths at me, they wag their
                   heads;"
Verse   8:   "He committed his cause to the
                   Lord; let him deliver him,
                   let him rescue him, for he delights in him!"
Verse 15:   "my strength is dried up like a potsherd,
                   and my tongue cleaves to my jaws;"
Verse 16:   ". . . they have pierced my hands and feet."
Verse 18:   "they divide my garments among them,
                   and for my raiment they cast lots."

To these the following parallels are found in the Gospel narratives:

To verse   7:   Matthew 27:39 and Mark 15:29 where the
                      "wagging of heads" is especially pointed out,
                      as well as other references to the mocking
                      of Jesus.
To verse   8:   Matthew 27:43, "He trusts in God; let God
                      deliver him now. . . ."
To verse 15:   John 19:28, "I thirst." Also Matthew 27:28;
                      Mark 15:36; and Luke 23:36 describe how
                      Jesus was offered a drink on the cross.
To verse 16:   Matthew 27:49 (according to several important manuscripts) and John 19:34. Both

add that water and blood came out of the
pierced side of Jesus.

To verse 18:   Matthew 27:35, ". . . they divided his garments among them by casting lots." See also
Mark 15:24; Luke 23:34; and John 19:23-24.

These similarities naturally bring up the critical question
as to whether or not the Gospel narratives were written
against the background of the Twenty-second Psalm. In other
words, did the early Christian community deliberately incor-
porate these instances of Psalm 22 into the passion narrative
and thus create points of "fulfillment" in the sufferings of
Jesus? Logical as this question may seem, it is scarcely possible. First of all, the passion narrative was the first of all the
Gospel stories; its roots must go back to eyewitness accounts.
It is difficult to believe that the early church would dare to
alter the accounts of eyewitnesses, adding to or detracting
from them to suit its theological objectives, when the fraud
would have been so easily discovered and exposed by others.

Secondly, this passion narrative was the most important
part of the primitive Christian tradition, and upon this the
entire proclamation of the Gospel was centered. Changing
any elements of this history would have been not only sacri-
legious but also quite dangerous to the Christian proclamation. If it could have been proved that historical events concerning the death of Jesus had been falsified by the Christians,
the whole movement could have been discredited. It is difficult to believe that any Christian would have taken this
chance. We must rather assume that all these things did take
place in the crucifixion — the mocking of Jesus, his thirst,
the piercing of his side, the division of his garments.

Further, since none of these things would be in any way
unusual at a public crucifixion, it was probably not the
passion narrative that was written against the background of
the Twenty-second Psalm, but vice versa: What actually

happened during the crucifixion reminded the followers of Jesus of the psalm. We may also conjecture that it was exactly what happened to him and around him during his crucifixion that recalled to the memory of Jesus himself the words of the Twenty-second Psalm, and for this reason he recited it. We need not consider these experiences to be the miraculous fulfillment of an Old Testament prophecy; and, strictly speaking, Psalm 22 is not a prophecy at all. Many of us have experienced a particular situation that may recall the words of a beloved poem or hymn so vividly that we recite it during our time of stress. For instance, a person may be painfully disappointed in a supposedly good friend; if this person is a Christian, he may remember the hymn, "What a Friend We Have in Jesus," and start to hum, or even to sing, the hymn because he feels that this hymn, especially its third stanza, speaks to his condition. Similarly, the Lord, in his hour of trial, remembered the words of the well-known Twenty-second Psalm, and he started to say it: "My God, my God, why hast thou forsaken me. . . ."

Also, beyond the external similarities, Psalm 22 has theological implications which were especially meaningful for Jesus' meditation in the hour of his death. Of greatest significance is the final climax of the psalm with its declaration of the eschatological breaking in of the kingdom of God. This feature is what drew Jesus' attention more than anything else in this psalm. The proclamation of the kingdom of God was his main mission. With it he started his preaching; it was the kingdom he sought to explain in sermons and parables. For the kingdom, he suffered persecution; and even the charge of his condemnation, written on his cross, called him a "king" of the Jews. Certainly Jesus did not merely claim to be an advocate of the messianic kingdom of God, but he also identified himself with the kingdom and made entirely dependent upon his own person the kingdom's coming and the individual's entry into it.

Did Jesus' death change anything in his teaching about the kingdom of God? By no means! It rather fulfilled it. In the death of Jesus the old age found its end and the new age its beginning. At the crucifixion the kingdom of God became a reality, and its doors were flung open. What Psalm 22 calls God's deliverance (v. 31) is now taking place. This is redemptive history in its making, and through the proclamation of this saving act of God faith in him will be stirred and his kingdom will grow beyond the limits of space and time. What we in our Good Friday services often call the "Words of Loneliness" are, in fact, words of triumph. The psalm climaxes in a wonderful victory song of the kingdom of God, and this refrain must have filled the mind of Jesus when he recited the last verses of this psalm:

> "All the ends of the earth shall remember
>   and turn to the Lord;
> and all the families of the nations
>   shall worship before him.
> For dominion belongs to the Lord,
>   and he rules over the nations.
>
> Yea, to him shall all the proud of
>   the earth bow down;
>   before him shall bow all who go
>   down to the dust,
>   and he who cannot keep himself alive.
> Posterity shall serve him;
>   men shall tell of the Lord to the
>   coming generation,
> and proclaim his deliverance to a
>   people yet unborn,
>   that he has wrought it."

"This man is calling Elijah. . . . Wait, let us see whether Elijah will come to save him."

'Ηλείας φωνεῖ οὖτος. . . . "Αφες ἴδωμεν εἰ ἔρχεται 'Ηλείας σώσων αὐτόν.

Why did the spectators around the cross of Jesus introduce the name of the prophet Elijah? The usual explanation is that they in their wickedness willfully distorted the words of Jesus and made "Elijah" out of "Eli" in order to ridicule him the more. This is possible (but by no means certain), and we must accept the possibility that the spectators made an honest mistake. "Eli" and "Elijah" are very close to each other in sound, and it is not difficult to mistake one for the other. Add to this the circumstances that prevailed at the time: The atmosphere was laden with messianic ideas, and the spectators were accustomed to thinking eschatologically. It is no wonder at all that the name of Elijah was used. In popular Jewish thinking, Elijah was supposed to return and introduce the Messiah. Even if Jesus had not uttered the words, "Eli, Eli . . . ," some of the Jews must have thought of the possibility that if the claim of Jesus were true, Elijah would appear and help him. So we can very well understand that when they heard Jesus saying something like "Eli, Eli . . . ," their minds almost automatically turned to the name of Elijah. They became even more excited than ever, and they said to each other: "He is calling Elijah! Let us wait and see whether Elijah will come and help him!" Elijah, of course, did not appear, and this circumstance was just another proof for the Jewish spectators that the messianic claim of Jesus was false. As anyone is apt to do, they interpreted the data in the light of their preconceptions.

Jewish eschatological expectations concerning Elijah were based upon the words of the prophet, Malachi 4:5-6 (3:23-24 in the Hebrew Bible) :

"Behold, I will send you Elijah the prophet before the great and terrible day of the Lord comes. And he will turn the hearts of fathers to their children and the hearts of children to their fathers, lest I come and smite the land with a curse."

The wonderful assumption of Elijah in the chariot of fire (2 Kings 2:11) quite naturally intrigued Jewish imagination. Elijah became the most popular biblical figure for the Jews, and around him many legends arose. He became something like a patron saint. His residence was thought to be Paradise, from whence he would come to help his people in time of need and trouble. As an eschatological figure, Elijah was expected to appear at the end of this age to prepare his people for the reception of the Messiah; he was to fight against the Anti-Christ and to reveal the Messiah. Elijah's popularity in New Testament times can be seen from the fact that reference is made to him in the four Gospels no less than twenty-seven times. Moses and Elijah are the ones who appear in the account of the transfiguration (Mark 9:4-5; Matthew 17:3-4; Luke 9:30-33) ; and John the Baptist will have ". . . the Spirit and power of Elijah . . ." (Luke 1:17). When the Samaritan villagers did not receive Jesus, James and John wanted to bring down fire to consume them as Elijah did (Luke 9:54). The idea of an eschatological return of Elijah was quite alive. Jesus himself was often identified by the people with Elijah. See the following texts: Mark 8:28; Matthew 16:14; Luke 9:19; Mark 6:15 (Luke 9:8) ; and John 1:21, 25. Elijah figured often in the conversation of Jesus with his disciples. For example, see Matthew 17:10 or Luke 4:25-26. Also, the Gospels show that Jesus himself accepted the prophecy concerning the return of Elijah. His answer was, of course, that this prophecy had been fulfilled and that Elijah had come in the person of John the Baptist (Matthew 11:14; 17:11-12; Mark 9:11-13) .

According to Matthew 7:12, Jesus once said: ". . . Elijah has already come, and they did not know him, but did to him whatever they pleased. So also the Son of Man will suffer at their hands." Those who did not recognize John the Baptist (probably the scribes and the religious leaders of Israel in general) were among the spectators on Golgotha. These leaders made a mistake, an honest mistake, but still a fateful mistake. They waited for the appearance of Elijah, but he had already come and had not been recognized. While they waited in vain for Elijah, they missed the Messiah himself, who was right in the midst of them reciting a victory-song to the kingdom of God (see Luke 17:21).

THE FIFTH WORD

John 19:28-29

▪▪▪

"After this Jesus, knowing that everything was now accomplished in order that the Scripture may be fulfilled, said: 'I thirst.' A bowl full of sour wine stood there, so they put a sponge full of the sour wine on hyssop and held it to his mouth" (author's translation) .

"After this Jesus, knowing that everything was now accomplished. . . ."

Μετὰ τοῦτο εἴδως ὁ Ἰησοῦς ὅτι ἤδη πάντα τετέλεσται. . . .

This passage brings us to the christological problem of the knowledge that Jesus possessed. The passage declares that Jesus KNEW that everything was now accomplished, or fulfilled. The form *eidōs* comes from *oida,* which means "to know," "to be intimately acquainted with." This meaning is similar to the one expressed by the very *ginōskō* from which the Gnostic movement received its name. Does this text reflect the Gnosticism which influenced the Fourth Gospel?

In no other book of the New Testament is the problem of knowledge dealt with so extensively as in the Fourth Gospel. This can be seen by the frequency of the use of the verbs *oida* and *ginōskō. Oida* occurs in the Fourth Gospel eighty-five times, in contrast to its infrequent use in the Synoptics — in Matthew, twenty-five times; in Mark, twenty-two; and in Luke, twenty-five times. *Ginosko* occurs in the Fourth

Gospel fifty-six times in contrast to its use in Matthew, twenty times; in Mark, twelve times; and in Luke, twenty-eight.[1] Of all these texts, only those which refer to the idea of knowing or not knowing God or Jesus Christ have theological significance. In this connection, the insufficient knowledge of the Pharisees, which arises from an acquaintance with the Law, is contrasted with the knowledge which comes from faith in Jesus Christ. In John 9:24 the Pharisees say to the formerly blind man: ". . . 'Give God the praise; we know that this man is a sinner.' " To this the man answers: "Whether he is a sinner, I do not know; one thing I know, that though I was blind, now I see" (John 9:25). Again, in verse 29 the Pharisees say to the man: "We know that God has spoken to Moses, but as for this man, we do not know where he comes from." The man's sarcastic answer exposes the Pharisees' empty shell of knowledge: "Why, this is a marvel! You do not know where he comes from, and yet he opened my eyes. WE KNOW that God does not listen to sinners, but if any one is a worshiper of God and does his will, God listens to him (John 9:30-31).

Similarly in John 3:2 the self-conscious assertion of the Pharisee Nicodemus, "WE KNOW that you are a teacher come from God," is rebuked by Jesus in verse 10 with these words: "Are you a teacher of Israel and yet YOU DO NOT KNOW this?" (author's trans.). The knowledge of the Pharisees is limited to an acquaintance with the words of the law given through Moses, but grace and truth came through Jesus Christ (John 1:17); and, therefore, in his words only are spirit and life (John 6:63). Since his coming, true knowledge of God is possible only through Jesus, and no one comes to the Father except by him (John 14:6). "If you had known me, you would have known my Father also; henceforth you know

---

[1] For a complete comparison, see Robert Morgenthaler, *Statistik des Neutestamentlichen Wortschatzes* (Zurich: Gotthelf-Verlag, 1958), pp. 85, 91.

him and have seen him" (John 14:7). Jesus Christ is able to give this knowledge because of his essential unity with God: "I know him, for I come from him . . ." (John 7:29). Therefore, when Philip said to him, "Lord, show us the Father," Jesus answered with these words: "Have I been with you so long, and yet you do not know ME?" (John 14:8. See also 8:19; 8:55-58; 10:14-18; etc.). Jesus Christ possesses a perfect knowledge of God, because he and God are one (John 10:30; 17:11).[2] In all these statements a Gnostic implication cannot be denied, but there is a basic difference from true Gnosticism as we shall soon observe. This emphasis upon special knowledge is not found in the Gospel of John only.

In all four Gospels a supernatural knowledge concerning human beings is attributed to Jesus Christ. It is reported several times that Jesus knew the unexpressed thoughts of the people and the unrevealed intentions of the Pharisees, and sometimes he even reacted to their thoughts before they asked him. (See Matthew 9:4; 12:25; Mark 12:15; Luke 11:17; John 6:61, 64.)

However, not until the disciples realized the unity of God and Jesus did they attribute a universal knowledge to Jesus: "Now we know that you know all things . . ." (John 16:30). In the appendix the same confession is repeated by Peter: "Lord, you know everything; you know that I love you" (John 21:17). The universal knowledge of Jesus included a knowledge of the redemptive purpose of God. Jesus knew why God sent him into the world. He knew about his future suffering and death, and he knew that the redemptive plan of God was to be realized perfectly in his suffering and death.

[2] See Heinrich Seesemann, article "oida," in Kittel, op. cit., vol. 5, pp. 116-119; Rudolph Bultmann, article "ginosko," in Kittel, op. cit., vol. 1, pp. 711ff. See Ethelbert Stauffer, Jesus and His Story (New York: Alfred A. Knopf, 1960), pp. 174ff; and J. Richter, "Ani Hu und Ego Eimi," Doctoral thesis, Erlangen, 1956, about an interesting hypothesis concerning the "I am" passages.

"Now before the feast of the Passover, when Jesus knew
that his hour had come to depart out of this world to the
Father. . . . And during supper . . . Jesus, knowing that the
Father had given all things into his hands, and that he had
come from God and was going to God . . ." (John 13:1-3).

"Then Jesus, knowing all that was to befall him, came forward and said to them, 'Whom do you seek?' " (John 18:4).

What, then, is meant by the remark of the Fourth Evangelist that Jesus, on the cross and close to death, knew "that
everything was now accomplished?" (author's trans.). What
did he know? He knew the plan of God, and he knew that
now everything was done and completely prepared for a perfect realization of the redemptive purpose of God. All was
prepared; the universe awaited salvation through the death
of the Son of God. This understanding of the sentence with
which we are dealing solves the problem concerning the
Gnostic influence attributed to it. The knowledge of Jesus is
not an abstract knowledge about God and his own existence,
but a knowledge of the plan of God, the realization of the
work for which he was sent, the obedience — the obedience
unto death — to the will of God. In contrast to the knowledge
of the Gnostics, which moves primarily in the vertical direc-
tion, the knowledge of Jesus Christ moves primarily on the
horizontal level of the history of redemption. In the last
analysis, it is the knowledge and the active affirmation of the
love of God, who "so loved the world that he gave his only
Son . . ." (John 3:16). For the followers of Jesus, knowledge
of God through him also means a relationship to God qualified and determined by this love. This knowledge is not
realized by mystic contemplation but in obedience to the
will of God in the concrete situations of the "here and now."

". . . in order that the Scripture may be fulfilled. . . ."

. . . *ἵνα τελειωθῇ ἡ γραφή.* . . .

The "Scripture" refers, of course, to the Old Testament, but it is not clear whether to a certain section, or to a specific prophecy, or to the witness of the Old Testament as a whole. If the former is the case, then the Scripture text is Psalm 69:21: "They gave me poison for food, and for my thirst they gave me vinegar to drink." In the Septuagint translation this verse is Psalm 68:22, where three key words are strongly reminiscent of John 19:28-29. These three words are *kholē, oxos,* and *dipsa.* Out of these three, however, only *oxos* is actually mentioned in the text of the Fourth Gospel. *Dipsa* appears in the form of *dipsō* (I thirst), and *kholē* is entirely missing, although it is used in Matthew 27:34. Nevertheless, the contents of the two texts are so similar to one another that some exegetes say that the Evangelist considered the condition of Jesus as the fulfillment of this psalm. In that case, the exegesis of this text is that Jesus cried for a drink because it was his desire to fulfill even the tiniest details of the prophecies concerning him. Then the "Scripture" means nothing more than this one verse of this psalm.

The situation, however, is not as simple as this. As a general rule, it may be said that when the New Testament refers to the whole Old Testament, or to the totality of the prophecies contained in it, then it uses the plural *hai graphai.* For example:

"Have you never read in the scriptures . . . ?" (Matthew 21:42).

"You are wrong, because you know neither the scriptures nor the power of God" (Matthew 22:29).

"You search the scriptures, because you think that in them you have eternal life" (John 5:39).

When a certain text or verse is meant, then the singular *graphai* is used. For example:

"Have you not read this scripture . . . ?" (Mark 12:10).

"He who believes in me, as the scripture has said, 'Out of his heart shall flow rivers of living water' " (John 7:38).

". . . it is that the scripture may be fulfilled, 'He who ate my bread has lifted his heel against me' " (John 13:18).

But these are only general rules; the practical use of singular and plural is by no means so consistent. Sometimes when the plural is used, only a single text of the Old Testament is meant, as in Matthew 21:42. Also, when the singular is used, often the whole Old Testament is meant, as in many texts in the Pauline letters and particularly in the following texts of the Fourth Gospel:

"When therefore he was raised from the dead, his disciples remembered that he had said this; and they believed the scripture and the word which Jesus had spoken" (John 2:22).

Here Scripture is singular, but it denotes the whole Old Testament because no reference is made to a particular passage.

". . . and scripture cannot be broken . . ." (John 10:35).

Here the RSV omits the article.

"While I was with them, I kept them in thy name which thou hast given me; . . . that the scripture might be fulfilled" (John 17:12).

Again, nothing is said about which Scripture might be fulfilled, and the reader has no other choice than to think of the whole Old Testament. The case of John 20:9 is similar:

"for as yet they did not know the scripture, that he must rise from the dead."

Thus, we are justified in saying that our text probably refers to the fulfillment of the whole Old Testament. The following arguments may be considered. In this text, as in the others which have been mentioned, no reference is made to a specific passage of the Old Testament. Psalm 69 is not mentioned in the Fourth Gospel. Also, if the author had this one psalm in mind, he possibly would have referred to it explicitly as he did in other cases. We must consider, too, that Psalm 69 does not fit into our text very well. The psalm speaks about men who out of malice do evil things to their neighbors, but in the Gospel the thirst of Jesus is simply quenched, without any malicious intent. In the subsequent verses of the psalm, the sufferer invokes the wrath of God upon his persecutors; in the Gospel there is no such idea connected with Jesus. The psalm speaks about "food" and "drink," but in the Gospel Jesus was not offered food on the cross, only drink. Therefore, no matter how suggestive Psalm 69 may seem, we would do better not to refer to it as a prophecy which was fulfilled in John 19:29.

In the Fourth Gospel the witness of Jesus to all the Old Testament writings is meant. The misinterpretation of this text comes from a very slight mistake in the reading of the verse. The verb "said" is usually connected with the preceding section "in order that the Scripture may be fulfilled," as if Jesus had said the words "I thirst" in order that a prophecy concerning him could find its fulfillment. This interpretation is wrong. The prophecies were already fulfilled, and nothing more was needed, as is clearly said in the first part of the sentence: "everything was now accomplished." This first part of the sentence must be related to the second, so that the meaning is: "everything is now accomplished, in order that the Scripture may be fulfilled; and Jesus, having seen this, said, 'I thirst!'" The work was done; and the thirst, which he had not felt before in his complete occupation with his Father's business, drove him to cry out for water.

"I thirst."

Διψῶ.

Several attempts have been made to explain this word. One hypothesis is, as we have just seen, that Jesus did not actually suffer from thirst but spoke this word only to fulfill prophecy. With slight modification, another theory says that Jesus did suffer thirst in order to fulfill a prophecy. Another hypothesis is that at this time Jesus reached a low point in his humiliation. He, who so confidently promised the "living water" to his followers (John 4:14; 6:35; 7:38), was himself in need of water. Again, another theory says that Jesus recited the Twenty-second Psalm only up to verse 15, and this was misheard or misinterpreted by the bystanders as a cry for water. This is very improbable. There is nothing in Psalm 22:15 that could be mistaken for "I thirst"; in verse 14 the word "water" occurs, but in another connection. Even so, it could not be misheard as, "I thirst." [3]

All these hypotheses suffer from one fault: They are all efforts to "explain," or to save Jesus Christ from the common experience of being thirsty. The incident does not fit into the image of Christ as an Apollo; and, consequently, men try to remove the sting from the whole incident. There is no need to do that because the humanity of Jesus is not something that we should try to tone down. Indeed, it cannot be toned down because the Gospel is so filled with it. Let us remember the passion narratives: In the garden of Gethsemane during the night of his arrest, he struggled with the idea of his execution. He tried to avoid all that was coming upon him! According to Luke 22:36-38, he even urged his disciples to buy some swords. When he saw that there was no possibility of escape, he still prayed to God, "Father, if thou art willing,

[3] Stauffer, *op. cit.,* pp. 140-141.

remove this cup from me . . ." (Luke 22:42). In all of these texts it is evident that Jesus was very human and not as anxious to be a hero as many people would like to picture him.

Nor was Jesus an ascetic. Pains in his body really made him suffer. The thought of his execution filled him with fear. He did not relish suffering. He did not enjoy being arrested and tortured. It was not easy for him to bear the cross. As a matter of fact, the cross was so heavy that Jesus collapsed under its weight, and another person, Simon from Cyrene, had to carry it for him. It was not easy for Jesus to be crucified, and his death on the cross was not a cheap sacrifice. Jesus never tried to hide his humanity. As far as the natural needs of his body, such as food and drink, were concerned, he lived quite a normal life. Just as there were those in his generation who held that he should conform to an ascetic pattern of life, some in our time hold to an ascetic image of Jesus. Jesus shrugged off any such suggestion with a simple sentence: "John came neither eating nor drinking, and they say, 'He has a demon'; the Son of Man came eating and drinking, and they say, 'Behold a glutton and a drunkard, a friend of tax collectors and sinners!' . . ." (Matthew 11:18-19). He did not deny his humanity on the cross. When he became thirsty, he asked for water. To understand this clearly, let us imagine the actual situation. The execution was accompanied by great bodily suffering. The wounds made by the nails caused terrible inflammations, and he was close to death. The condition of Jesus was somewhat similar to that of soldiers fatally wounded in a battle who often ask for water before they die. But even in a hospital, when patients run a temperature, or after an operation when the mouth and the lips of a patient become parched and dry, a few drops of water often suffice for temporary relief. Jesus suffered; his mouth was dry; his lips were parched; the wounds were inflamed; his blood was running; his vision may have been already blurred; and he said, probably in a weak, almost inaudible voice, "I thirst."

"A bowl full of sour wine stood there. . . ."

σκεῦος ἔκειτο ὄξους μεστόν. . . .

The meaning of *oxos* is not necessarily vinegar, but cheap, inferior, sour grape wine. It was a popular drink, especially among soldiers and laborers, because it was refreshing and thirst-quenching. With more acid content, however, it was also used in the preparation of food, and thus it served as vinegar. Physicians sometimes prescribed it to bring down body temperature and as a general stimulant.[4] To decide now whether this drink was vinegar or wine, we must rely upon our imagination. Was it likely that anyone would carry a bowl of vinegar up to the place of an execution? Why would anyone do such a thing? The Lucan and Johannine accounts say that it was a part of the mockery that Jesus was offered vinegar, and the humor apparently would be that a person tasting vinegar usually makes a grimace, a semi-comic face that causes other people to laugh. This is hard to believe for two reasons. First, if anyone did carry vinegar up to the place of the execution for this sole purpose, he could not be sure that Jesus would ask for a drink. According to the Gospel narratives, drink was given to him because he did expressly ask for it, in contrast to the other two men on the crosses who did not. Secondly, in the next verse we read that Jesus actually took the drink that was offered to him, which means that it must have been a kind of drink that he could enjoy. If it had been vinegar, he probably would have refused to take it, as he had refused to take the narcotic drink that was offered to him.

[4] Hans W. Heidland in Kittel, *op. cit.,* vol. 5, pp. 288-289.

To understand the situation completely, we must know that crucifixion was a special Roman way of execution, and it was carried out by Roman soldiers. At that time in Israel the Sanhedrin was denied the power to carry out a death sentence, although it could pass such a sentence. Therefore, the actual execution of Jesus was a Roman affair. A crucifixion was nothing new or exciting for the Romans, but a rather common thing. Josephus tells us that Roman procurators in Palestine sometimes crucified whole multitudes. On one occasion the procurator Felix arrested and executed a robber chief, Eleazar, and many of his bandsmen, who "were a multitude not to be numbered." [5] They were all crucified. Josephus also writes about the procurator Florus, who made a massacre in Jerusalem: ". . . they also caught many of the quiet people, and brought them before Florus, whom he first chastised with stripes, and then crucified. Accordingly, the whole number of those that were destroyed that day . . . was about three thousand and six hundred." [6] Thus, we may conjecture that, to the soldiers who were in charge, the execution of three persons was not a particularly entertaining event. Since they passed the time by casting lots, they were probably bored. It is quite probable that these soldiers brought some cheap wine with them to the place of execution with the thought that while they waited there, and it sometimes took several hours, they would drink the wine. What these soldiers would bring, of course, would be wine and not vinegar, and Jesus was given a drink from their supply of wine. We conclude, therefore, that this drink was wine, and it was given to Jesus not as an act of mockery but rather of kindness.

This drink, which Jesus asked for and accepted, must be distinguished from the one that was offered to him before

[5] "Wars of the Jews," *The Life and Works of Flavius Josephus,* William Whiston, trans. (Philadelphia: The John C. Winston Company, n.d.), book 2, chap. 13, par. 2.

[6] *Ibid.,* chap. 14, par. 9.

he was put on the cross. In Matthew 27:34 the drink is called "wine . . . mingled with gall *(kholē),*" and in Mark 15:23 it is ". . . wine mingled with myrrh." The discrepancy between the two texts is slight since *kholē* does not always mean gall, but in a more general sense it simply means something bitter, which was the taste of myrrh when mingled with wine. The purpose of this drink was to stupefy the condemned man, and it was a general Jewish practice to do this to all persons who were led to execution. We have many references to this in the Jewish literature. In a tractate of the Talmud Sanhedrin 43/a: "Rab Chisda said, To him who went out to be executed a piece of incense was given in a cup of wine, in order to make him unconscious." [7] This custom is based in the Jewish literature upon Proverbs 31:6: "Give strong drink to him who is perishing, and wine to those in bitter distress." It is also recorded that the prominent women of Jerusalem used to donate this drink; and only if they refused to give it freely, was it to be paid for by the congregation. This old custom may be the basis of Ethelbert Stauffer's suggestion that "the leading women of Jerusalem met the party and gave them a jug of wine in which narcotic essences had been steeped." [8] Actually, we do not know whether or not this happened in the case of Jesus' crucifixion since the women mentioned in Luke 23:27 are wailing women, and the "many women" at the cross mentioned by Matthew 27:55 are followers of Jesus. Regardless of who paid for the drink, it was at hand; and sometime before the execution it was offered to Jesus to make him unconscious, but he refused to take it. Could this narcotizing drink, which was available at the place of execution, have been offered to Jesus the second time when he

[7] Herman L. Strack and Paul Billerbeck, *Kommentar zum Neuen Testament aus Talmud und Midrash* (Munchen: C. H. Beck'sche Verlagsbuchhandlung, Oscar Beck, 1922), vol. 1, p. 1037. Here are numerous other references from the rabbinic literature concerning this custom.

[8] Stauffer, *op. cit.,* p. 135.

asked for a drink? The answer is no, because the evangelists make a definite distinction between the two drinks. The first time it was a narcotizing drink; the second time it probably was sour wine, which had been brought to the scene by the soldiers for their own use.

"... *so they put a sponge ... on hyssop.* ..."

... σπογγον οὖν ... ὑσσώπω περιθέντες. ...

This text is a *crux theologorum* because it implies that hyssop is a plant which would have a stalk long and strong enough to support a sponge filled with wine and to reach up to the mouth of a person hanging on the cross. But hyssop is a small bush, and its stems do not grow higher than one or one and one half feet. If the cross were not too high, the stem would be long enough. The difficulty arises when we compare the Johannine account with Matthew and Mark and discover that these two Gospels say nothing of hyssop and mention only *kalamos,* which means a reed or a stalk. It may even mean a measuring rod or a reed pen.[9] Did the author of the Fourth Gospel have a special purpose in introducing the idea of the hyssop in connection with the death of Jesus? Hyssop in the Old Testament indicates a purifying effect: "Purge me with hyssop, and I shall be clean. . ." (Psalm 51:7). Before the Exodus the Israelites were commanded to kill the passover lamb, then to "Take a bunch of hyssop and dip it in the blood . . . and touch the lintel and the two doorposts with the blood. . ." (Exodus 12:22). Similarly, in Leviticus 14:4 and Numbers 19:6, 18, hyssop is used to sprinkle the cleansing blood. Hebrews 9 explains that the sacrifice of Christ is the real sacrifice which was prefigured in the Mosaic

[9] Walter A. Bauer, *A Greek-English Lexicon of the New Testament and Other Early Christian Literature.*

rites, and Hebrews 19:19 mentions the hyssop with which the blood was sprinkled. Thus, it is not impossible that the Fourth Evangelist introduced the idea of hyssop to accent the sacrificial character of the death of Jesus and to be a reminder of the passover lamb.

Joachim Camerarius (1500-1574), a friend of Melanchthon and a great commentator and scholar of the sixteenth century, was the first one to suggest that the original text may have had *hussō* instead of *hussōpō*. Actually, there is one minuscule, No. 476, which reads this way. *Hussos* means "lance," and in that case, the meaning would be that they put the sponge on a lance instead of on a hyssop or reed. Unfortunately, there is only this one minuscule which supports Camerarius' interpretation. From the point of view of the textual critic, this is insufficient. But we cannot let the matter rest because Camerarius' suggestion is very plausible and has been accepted by many modern exegetes. If we compare the two possibilities with each other, we will almost automatically decide upon the "lance." The Roman soldiers could have, and very probably did have, lances around. One of them would be long enough to reach up to the mouth of Jesus. It would also be strong enough to carry a sponge filled with wine. The same thing could not be said of hyssop, or even a reed. Inasmuch as it is not very difficult to write *hussōpō* instead of *hussō,* it is possible that "hyssop" came into the text as a mistake in a very early transcription of the Gospel. If the Fourth Evangelist did not put in "hyssop" himself because of its symbolic connotations (a possibility which is discounted by many scholars including Bultmann), then our best and most logical choice is to substitute "lance" for "hyssop." This correction makes the understanding of the text much easier.

Another observation is that apparently the cross on which Jesus hung was so high that the soldier had to use some extension device to reach his mouth. Hence, those who mocked Jesus called on him to ". . . come DOWN from the cross" (Mark 15:30, 32; Matthew 27:40). The feet of Jesus may have been about three or four feet from the ground, so that he was high enough to be seen by a great number of people, even from a distance. We know that not all crosses were so high because people were put on crosses in the Roman circus and exposed to the attacks of wild animals. Then, of course, the crosses which were used must have been lower. Why a higher cross was used for Jesus we do not know, but it is significant to know that the passion and the death of Jesus could be seen easily by many people. We may assume that the passion narratives give us an accurate report because the writers would not and could not falsify the account of an historical event which was witnessed by many people who could contradict the account if it were in error.

". . . so they put a sponge full of the sour wine on hyssop and held it to his mouth."

. . . σπογγον οὖν μεστὸν τοῦ ὄξους ὑσσώπω περιθέντες προσήνεγκαν αὐτοῦ τῷ στόματι.

The writer of the Fourth Gospel does not say who offered the drink to Jesus. He simply uses the third person plural. Similarly, Mark says that "some of the bystanders" heard the cry of Jesus, and "one ran" and gave Jesus the drink. Matthew uses almost the same words as Mark, but Luke 23:36 mentions the soldiers: "The soldiers also mocked him, coming up and offering him sour wine" (author's trans.). As Matthew, Mark, and John do not contradict Luke, it seems that one of the soldiers gave the drink. Because the thing on which the sponge was placed was probably not a reed but a javelin or lance, which would have been the property of the Romans, it is improbable that anyone other than a soldier would be permitted to handle it. Also, it is very improbable that anyone from the crowd of bystanders would be allowed to touch the victims. In Semach 2, 9, concerning those who were led to execution, it is related that they were permitted to talk to their brothers and relatives only, and only then in so far as it did not delay the course of events.[10] Therefore, it is difficult to imagine that anyone from the crowd could give Jesus the drink. Even the ecclesiastical authorities would not be permitted to interfere with the Roman execution. The activities of the Jewish bystanders and the priest were probably limited to deriding him and "wagging their heads." The mocking was done by the Jews; the drink was given by a Roman soldier.

According to Mark 15:36, while the soldier gave this drink to Jesus, he said these words: "Wait, let us see whether Elijah will come to take him down." These words of the soldier raise the following questions: To whom is he talking, and what does he mean by the word "wait"? One hypothesis says that he is talking to the other soldiers who tried to stop him from giving the wine to Jesus.[11] It would be perhaps easier to assume that he was talking to the people and especially to the mockers. There was probably much noise and great disorder in the crowd. Some said, "You who would destroy the temple and build it in three days, save yourself . . ."; the priests and scribes said, "He saved others, he cannot save himself. . . ." Even one of the criminals crucified with him shouted at him. Naturally, all these things were not said one after the other, but in great disorder. Undoubtedly, much more was said than the evangelists deemed necessary to write down. It is also possible that some of the people or the priests resented the soldier's giving the drink to Jesus, and it was this shouting, excited, disorderly mob to whom the soldier spoke.

[10] Strack-Billerbeck, *op. cit.,* vol. 1, p. 1037.

[11] M. J. Lagrange, *The Gospel of Jesus Christ* (Westminster, Md.: The Newman Press, 1943) , vol. 2, p. 272.

When he heard one of them saying, "Behold, he is calling Elijah," the soldier used this idea to try to quiet the mob. His words may have had this simple meaning: "Be quiet; don't shout; wait a little; see if Elijah is coming to help him!"

Giving the drink was an act of kindness on the part of the soldier who, when he heard or when he thought he heard Jesus cry, "I thirst," put a sponge at the end of his lance, dipped it in the jug of wine, which was beside him, and held it up to the mouth of Jesus. Why did he do it? No one will ever be able to say because no one can know what goes on in the secret chambers of a human soul. Perhaps he was one of those who later said, "Truly this was the son of God!" (Matthew 27:54). Or perhaps he had a sudden impulse, a surge of pity in his heart. In any case, this is certainly one of the most touching scenes on Golgotha, and it is impossible not to remember the eschatological words of Jesus: "Come, O blessed of my Father, inherit the kingdom prepared for you . . . for I was thirsty and you gave me drink . . ." (Matthew 25:34-35).

THE SIXTH WORD

John 19:30

"When Jesus had received the sour wine, he said: 'It is accomplished' . . ." (author's translation).

"It is accomplished." (1)

Τετέλεσται

This word from the cross can be understood best by considering its meaning from three different perspectives: (1) as a part of the Jewish evening prayer, (2) as a verb form with particular grammatical significance, and (3) as a term with definite theological meaning.

In the Gospel accounts, all four evangelists agree that before Jesus breathed his last, he uttered certain words. Although Mark and Matthew do not give these words (they mention only "a loud cry"), Luke asserts that the words were, "Father, into thy hands I commit my spirit!" (Luke 23: 46). The Fourth Evangelist says that these last words were, "It is accomplished." If one assumes that the words spoken from the cross, as they are recorded in the Gospel narratives, were single sentences or exclamations without any logical connection with each other, then the question arises as to which account, the Lucan or the Johannine, has recorded the last words correctly. Such an assumption, although it is quite popular today, seems to me to be incorrect. I shall attempt to show that both of these sentences were parts of a longer utterance of Jesus. What Jesus actually said on the cross before he breathed his last was the customary Jewish evening prayer with a specific addition for Friday night.

At least two of the seven words of Jesus from the cross were taken from the Psalms: Psalm 22:1 and Psalm 31:5. Whether Jesus spoke only these single verses, or whether he recited the whole psalm in each case, is a question which must be raised in the light of the fact that the eyewitnesses of the crucifixion could not possibly hear and understand all that Jesus said. His prayers were probably murmured in a low voice, which was not an extraordinary way for Jews to pray. Possibly the Marcan eyewitness could not understand the loud cry Jesus uttered before his death, because the circumstances were such that it was difficult to understand it. We therefore assume that the eyewitnesses reported correctly what they heard, but there were words they could not hear or understand. In addition, they probably did not record every single word Jesus actually uttered. In the case of the Twenty-second Psalm we may assume that Jesus recited not only the first verse but the following verses also and possibly the whole psalm. In the case of the Thirty-first Psalm the logical conclusion is that he also recited the whole psalm.

It is well known that a part of the evening prayer recommended for Friday night was from Genesis. In Schabbath 119b we read the following:

> Rab Chisda (died 309) said that Mar Uqba (around 220) said: When someone prays on the evening before the Sabbath and speaks the words of Genesis 2:1 "Thus the heavens and the earth were finished, etc." then the two angels, which accompany men, will place their hands upon his head and they will speak to him: "Your guilt is taken away, and your sin forgiven." [1]

[1] Herman L. Strack and Paul Billerbeck, *Kommentar zum Neuen Testament aus Talmud und Midrash,* vol. 3, p. 781.

Since this reference goes back to the year 220, it is certain that its roots go back much farther. This custom is still today observed by the Jewish communities, and the Genesis text is repeated every Friday evening. Moreover, when the Passover falls upon a Friday, Genesis 1:31—2:1-3 is added to the regular Passover liturgy. The complete prayer follows:

> And it was evening and it was morning. The sixth day, the heavens, the earth, and all their hosts were finished. God finished on the seventh day the work which He had made, and He rested on the seventh day from all his work which He had made. And God blessed the seventh day and made it holy, because on it He rested from all His work which He created and made.[2]

The Hebrew verb *kalah* (to be completed, finished, accomplished) occurs in this prayer twice; and it is possible that these were the two words which were heard clearly and recorded by the source of the Fourth Gospel.[3]

For the correct exegesis of these words, we should know in what language they were uttered originally. The mother language of Jesus was undoubtedly Aramaic, but we have good reason to believe that he could converse in Greek and was acquainted also with Hebrew. It is almost impossible to decide which language he used on the cross. In the case of the Twenty-second Psalm, it was probably the original Hebrew. In the case of his asking for water, it may have been Aramaic. When he prayed, he could have spoken in Aramaic (which was officially permitted), or he could have recited the original Hebrew version. Dalman assumes that "It is accomplished" was said in Aramaic, and consequently he translates it with *mushlam*. However, Franz Delitzsh in his Hebrew translation of the New Testament uses the verb *kulla* which sounds very similar to the *vajjekullu* of Genesis 2:1.[4] Very pos-

[2] *Passover Haggadah* (New York: Ktav Publishing House, 1956), p. 5.

[3] Ethelbert Stauffer, *Jesus and His Story*, p. 141.

[4] Gustaf Dalman, *Jesus-Jeshua; Studies in the Gospels*, Paul Levertoff, trans. (New York: The Macmillan Company, 1929), p. 211.

sibly *vajjekullu* may be the word Jesus actually said, but it reached the ears of the eyewitnesses as *kulla* and became fixed as that in oral tradition. That Jesus used the Greek *tetelestai* as it stands in the Fourth Gospel is quite improbable. The verb in this Greek form is a translation of the original Hebrew, and it is molded to fit the theological purposes of the Fourth Evangelist. Thus, instead of *sunetelesthēsan* or *sunetelesen,* as in the Greek translation of Genesis 2:1-2, he put *tetelestai.*

It seems quite plausible, therefore, that the last words of Jesus were the words of an evening prayer. Elements of this prayer may have been Psalm 31:5, which was recommended as a general evening prayer, and Genesis 2:1, which was used Friday nights. The discrepancy between the Lucan and the Johannine accounts comes from the fact that one tradition reported the words of Psalm 31 and the other the two significant verbs of Genesis 2:1. Apart from the historical fact that Jesus Christ did speak from the cross, the word *tetelestai* seems to be especially important for the Fourth Evangelist. In fact, within the total framework of the Fourth Gospel, this word constitutes a climax full of theological implications. We can understand the meaning of this word only within the whole theology of the Fourth Gospel and not just within the historical context in which the word was spoken. This principle holds true for everything in the Fourth Gospel, but it has a particular significance in connection with the passion narrative, which is its heart.

"It is accomplished." (2)

Τετέλεσται

The verb *teleō* is used here in the passive perfect indicative, which is very difficult to translate into English accurately, because the perfect tense in Greek combines both present and aorist. It denotes a present condition which is the result of a past action. When Paul says in Romans 8:38 *pepeismai,* he speaks about his present state of mind which is a result of past experiences. When *gegraptai* is used in the New Testament to refer to the Old Testament, this word means that something now stands written, as a result of its having been written in the past. We must bear in mind this peculiar character of the perfect tense if we want to understand the correct meaning of this word from the cross.

Teleō (similar to *teleioō*) means to bring to an end, to accomplish. The noun derived from the verb is *telos,* which means "end," either as the cessation of something, ". . . of his kingdom there will be no end" (Luke 1:33), or as the goal of something, "its end is to be burned" (Hebrews 6:8). Bauer describes the second meaning as the objective "toward which a movement is being directed." [5] Romans 10:4 can be translated in both ways: the end of the law is Christ, either in the sense that with him the law ceases, or in the sense that the law pointed toward and educated for Christ. *Teleō* has the same connotations: It means to bring to an end, either in the sense of finishing, completing, "I have finished the race," (2 Timothy 4:7), or in the sense of bringing something to its goal and accomplishment. In this sense the verb is related to *plēroō,* which means to fill, to bring something to its full measure, to fulfill. It is interesting to note that, although the Fourth Gospel uses both verbs, the author shows a definite preference for *plēroō,* which he uses fifteen times, in contrast to *teleō* and *teleioō,* which he uses seven times. Especially when he speaks about the Scripture that was fulfilled, the verb is always *plēroō* (John 12:38; 13:18; 15:25; 17:12; 18:9; 19:24, 36). The only exception is 19:28 where *teleioō* is the verb, apparently because the *tetelestai* of verse

[5] Walter A. Bauer, *A Greek-English Lexicon of the New Testament and Other Early Christian Literature,* p. 819.

30 should be emphasized. Perhaps the evangelist also tried to prevent his readers from thinking in terms of *plēroō* only, because at this particular point the important thing is the idea of the *telos*: a certain goal has been achieved, a development has been brought to its successful end, a purpose has found its realization. The idea is not just simply "fulfilled" *(plēroō)*, as an empty space or an empty container is filled up, nor as the number of certain days or certain specific requirements can be "fulfilled." The death of Jesus Christ is infinitely more meaningful and more significant because it is the end, the purpose, and the final cause of a whole age in the history of redemption.

The use of the perfect tense indicates that a present condition that is the result of past actions is described here. Something exists; something is in effect now which did not exist before because certain actions have been taken. In this one word the whole theology of the history of redemption is condensed. When this word was spoken, one age was closed, and a new one began.

"It is accomplished." (3)

Τετέλεσται

Now we must examine the theological meaning of this word as it was conceived of by the Fourth Evangelist. This author, whoever he may have been, was not satisfied merely to record historical events; he wanted to write a book in which all historical events would be related within a theological framework. When he wrote, "It is accomplished," he must have had certain things in mind which, according to his theology, were accomplished by the death of Jesus.

The mission of Jesus Christ is accomplished. What was the mission of Jesus? It was to do the work of God (John 9:3-4;

10:37). Jesus was sent by God to accomplish something in the world, to bring the work of God in the world to its goal. Many times in the Fourth Gospel Jesus used the same word, "accomplish," in connection with the work of God that he was to do — "My food is to do the will of him who sent me, and to accomplish his work" (John 4:34) ; ". . . the works which the Father has granted me to accomplish, these very works which I am doing, bear me witness that the Father has sent me" (John 5:36). What works of God did Jesus mean? The works of manifesting the name of God to the world (John 17:6). The works of planting the love of God into the hearts of men: "I made known to them thy name, and I will make it known, that the love with which thou hast loved me may be in them, and I in them" (John 17:26). Jesus completed his task. Just before the passion narratives, the Fourth Gospel reports Jesus saying, "I glorified thee on earth, having accomplished the work which thou gavest me to do" (John 17:4). In all these texts the verb *teleioō* is used for "accomplish." Then, on the cross and near death, Jesus, as if he were looking back upon his life, said, "It is accomplished!" The work was done, the mission over.

The redemptive plan of God is accomplished. The will of God not to leave the world under the power of sin but to save it and regain it for himself has been successfully carried out. It was the conviction of the entire primitive Christian community, as reflected in the Synoptics and the Fourth Gospel, that the writings of the Old Testament found their meaning in Christ, that all that was said and hoped for concerning a Messiah was fulfilled in the life and mission, in the death and resurrection of Jesus Christ. Moses had spoken of him (John 5:46), and Abraham had rejoiced in him (John 8:56). Beginning from his conception (Matthew 1:22) up until his death (John 19:36-37) and resurrection (John 20:9), everything happened in order to fulfill the Scripture (John 19:36). Everything had been written beforehand. Everything had been prophesied and prefigured. Jesus Christ was not an accident in world history. He was in the eternally predestined plan of God for the redemption of the world. The belief of the Christian community that his death was not a mistake that could have been avoided found its most eloquent expression in the Pentecostal sermon of Peter:

> "Men of Israel, hear these words: Jesus of Nazareth, a man attested to you by God with mighty works and wonders and signs which God did through him in your midst, as you yourselves know — this Jesus, delivered up according to the definite plan and foreknowledge of God, you crucified and killed by the hands of lawless men" (Acts 2:22-23).

That the fulfillment of all these things was not an accident was declared from the cross with this one word *tetelestai;* the predestined plan of God had achieved its *telos.*

Nothing would be more contrary to the spirit of this text than to feel frustration in the word of Jesus, a shattering of all hopes, as if he had said, "It is finished! That is the end!" This word from the cross brings no premonition of immediate death, as if Jesus had said, "This is the end!" The verbs *teleō* and *teleioō* are used three times in the short section of John 19:28, 29, 30. At one of these times *teleioō* is even used in an expression in which the Fourth Evangelist otherwise always used *plēroō:* ". . . Jesus knowing that all was now accomplished in order that the Scripture may be fulfilled . . . said, 'It is accomplished . . .'" (author's trans.). The intention of the Evangelist is clear: It is already the exalted Christ who is speaking, and he speaks with authority as one who just entered upon his new and high office, as one who just began his kingly rule. This statement is the conqueror's proclamation of victory at the end of the battle.

What Jesus had accomplished was the inauguration of the new age. The death of Jesus Christ meant not merely an end, but also a beginning. Thus, the death of Jesus Christ became the true center of history. On one hand, it was the culmination of a development and the end of an age; but, on the other hand, it was the point where new events had their beginning and a new age started. When we understand this correctly, a new light is shed upon all former statements of Jesus in which he said that his "time" or his "hour" had NOT YET come. We see that in the Fourth Gospel the author gradually and very consciously builds up this tension of timing in the life of Jesus. At the beginning the time is NOT YET; but, as the story of the passion proceeds, the key word is NOW; and the climax is reached in the cry, "IT IS ACCOMPLISHED!"

In John 2:4 Jesus said to Mary, "What is it to you or to me, O woman? My hour has not yet come" (author's trans.). In the light of the *tetelestai,* we understand that he meant this specific hour of his death as the time of his glorification when the real miracle would be performed. Everything that he was doing then, before the cross, pointed to his death and could be understood only in the light of his death.

In the light of his anticipated sacrificial death, the wine at Cana also receives its true significance. Also, pointing toward his death, Jesus said to his brothers: ". . . I am not going up to this feast, for my time has not yet fully come" (John 7:8). In 7:30 and 8:20 we read that no one arrested him "because his hour was not yet come" (KJV). However, as the messianic work of Jesus unfolds, the "not yet" gradually changes to a proleptic "now." "The hour is coming," said Jesus to the Samaritan woman in 4:23, "and now is, when the true worshipers will worship the Father in spirit and truth. . . ." Similarly in 5:25, "the hour is coming, and now is, when the dead will hear the voice of the Son of God, and those who hear will live."

As we approach the time of the last Passover when ". . . Jesus knew that his hour had come . . ." (John 13:1), the futuristic "is coming" no longer figures in the pronouncements of Jesus. "Now is the judgment of this world, now shall the ruler of this world be cast out," Jesus said in John 12:31. "Now is the Son of man glorified, and in him God is glorified" (John 13:31). And just before the passion narrative, in 17:5, Jesus prayed, ". . . and now, Father, glorify thou me in thy own presence. . . ." It is interesting to observe that the adverbs "not yet," "now," and "already" are more often used by the Fourth Evangelist than in the Synoptics.

		Matthew	Mark	Luke	John
oupō	(not yet)	2	4	1	12
nun	(now)	4	3	14	28
arti	(now)	7	..	..	12
ede	(already)	7	8	10	16

The significance of these adverbs is chronological in the sense that they prepare and lead up to the time of the death of Jesus, which the Fourth Evangelist calls "that hour" (19:27). Not merely the chronological sequence of events is indicated by these adverbs, but rather their use is conditioned by a theological consideration of the Fourth Evangelist. "That hour," that tremendous "now" on Golgotha, declares the reality of salvation already in this world. The Evangelist is quite aware of the fact that sin and death still continue, that the return of Christ still must be awaited. Until the time of the Parousia, the old age and the new age overlap each other; and this overlapping of ages is the time for the existence of the Christian church, which was perceived at the cross by the beloved disciple, who "from that hour" took Mary, the representative of the old covenant, to his own home. In the Christian church there is an anticipation of the Parousia, the resurrection of the dead, and the kingdom of God. In the cross all of the apocalyptic expectations of the people of the old covenant about the coming of the Messiah have become reality because the death of Jesus inaugurated a new age. The immensely important matter which is being declared from the cross is that this turning of the course of history has been accomplished. It is a fact now, *tetelestai!*

THE SEVENTH WORD

Luke 23:46

||||||||||||||||||||||||||||||||||||||||||||||||||||||||||||||||||||||||||||||||

"Then Jesus, crying with a loud voice, said, 'Father, into thy hands I commit my spirit!' And having said this he breathed his last."

Before discussing the seventh, and final, word from the cross, it would be appropriate to consider the extraordinary events which surrounded the death of Jesus according to the reports of the Synoptic Gospels. These events took place immediately before or after his death, but not all of these miracles are reported by all three evangelists:

1. Darkness over the land
2. The torn curtain of the temple
3. An earthquake (in Matthew only)
4. Partial resurrection of the dead (in Matthew only)

Speaking in general terms, miraculous events accompanying the deaths of important personalities were by no means unusual in ancient literature. According to the rabbinic literature, there were a number of occasions when extraordinary things happened at the death of famous rabbis. For instance, when a rabbi died in the daytime, the stars became visible; and many similar miracles occurred.[1] These miracles, of

---

[1] Herman L. Strack and Paul Billerbeck, *Kommentar zum Neuen Testament aus Talmud und Midrash,* vol. 1, pp. 1040-1041.

course, served merely as a means of expressing the greatness
or the importance of the person involved, or perhaps they
pointed out the basic character of the decedent. Thus, from
a purely literary point of view, the reporting of miracles at
the death of Jesus was quite in accordance with the practice
of ancient authors, although the question of historical reality
must be left open in many instances.

1. *The darkness over the land.* The darkness is reported
by all three evangelists in the following manner:

"Darkness over the whole land" (Mark 15:33).

"Darkness over all the land" (Matthew 27:45).

". . . darkness over the whole land . . . while the sun's
light failed" (Luke 23:44).

First, the meaning of the word "land" must be clarified.
The Greek word used in the Gospels is *gē,* which can mean
both "land" and "earth." This ambiguity gave rise to the
speculation whether the darkness covered the whole earth, or
only the land of Palestine. The question can be answered
easily. The Greek *gē* is the same as the Hebrew word *eres.*
In common usage this word meant the land of Israel, so the
authors of the Synoptic Gospels probably meant that the darkness covered the territory of Palestine only. Second, Luke
attributes the darkness to an eclipse, which could not have
been the case, because the Passover fell at the time of the
full moon. However, astronomical arguments cannot exclude
the possibility of a darkness at noon, which could have been
caused by other elements than an eclipse, such as, a gathering
storm, or an unusually heavy cloud formation. Merely because an eclipse of the sun was impossible at the time of the
death of Jesus, one cannot say that the darkness as described
by the Synoptics did not actually take place.

Yet, the Synoptic Gospels' purpose was not merely to report
an historical event independent of the theological implica-

tions of the death of Jesus. In the passion narratives the darkness is referred to in a manner which clearly indicates that this phenomenon of nature was in direct connection with what was taking place on the cross. The following quotations from the Old Testament may make this clear:

". . . Behold, by my rebuke. . . .
I clothe the heavens with blackness,
    and make sackcloth their covering."
                                    Isaiah 50:2-3

"The sun and the moon are darkened,
    and the stars withdraw their shining."
                                    Joel 2:10

" 'And on that day,' says the Lord God,
    'I will make the sun go down at noon,
    and darken the earth in broad daylight.' "
                                    Amos 8:9

Compare also Matthew 24:29. The darkness, therefore, is a response of God to the events of Good Friday, by which he expresses his anger over the sinful practices of men. At the same time, however, the darkness is a sign of the fulfillment of his promise concerning "his day." It is not only "a day of darkness and gloom, a day of clouds and thick darkness!" (Joel 2:2), but also the beginning of the eschatological time when God will pour out his Spirit on all flesh (Joel 2:28). In the passion narrative of the Synoptics, the darkness identifies Good Friday as the "day of the Lord," as a messianic time; and the death of Jesus is thus characterized as having eschatological significance.

2. *The curtain of the temple.* The incident of the rending of the temple veil is reported by the Synoptics in the following ways:

"The curtain of the temple was torn in two, from top to bottom" (Mark 15:38; Matthew 27:51).

"The curtain of the temple was torn in two" (Luke 23:45b).

According to Josephus, there were two veils in the temple: one before the so-called "holy place," and the other before the "Holy of Holies." [2] This second curtain is the one which is referred to in Exodus 26:33, ". . . the veil shall separate for you the holy place from the most holy." There can be no doubt that the Gospel writers had this curtain in mind, and not the first one, which had no particular significance at all. Moreover, Hebrews 6:19; 9:3; and 10:20 clearly refer to the second curtain, which plays such an important role in the theology of that letter. Was the rending of the curtain an historical fact, or does it have only a symbolic meaning?

Concerning the historical question, in addition to the reports of the Synoptics, there are two literary sources which give some help. The first one is the rabbinic literature in which several references can be found concerning Jewish traditions about strange things which took place in the temple forty years before its destruction. Without any apparent reason, the light of a lamp suddenly went out; one night a very heavy door, which was carefully closed in the evening, was mysteriously opened; and several more similar events are described.[3] Secondly, Josephus also mentions that before the Jewish rebellion many strange things happened in the temple and in Jerusalem. For example: a comet appeared over the city for a whole year; a heifer gave birth to a lamb in the middle of the temple as she was led by the priest to be sacrificed; a door opened itself at night; one night an exceedingly great light was seen around the altar; at the feast of Pentecost, when the priests went into the inner court, they felt an earthquake accompanied with noise; and other mys-

---

[2] "Wars of the Jews," *The Life and Works of Flavius Josephus,* William Whiston, trans., book 5, chap. 5, par. 4-5, p. 784.

[3] Strack-Billerbeck, *op. cit.,* vol. 1, pp. 1045-1046.

terious things happened.[4] As Jerusalem and the temple were destroyed in 70 A.D., forty years before that event would be 30 A.D., which was approximately the time of Jesus. The happenings described by Josephus and the rabbinic literature are very similar in nature to the tearing of the curtain. This argument does not decide the historical question beyond doubt, but it is still important to know that traditions similar to the tearing of the curtain were current among the Jews in the time of Josephus and even later.

Even if it were not an historical event, the rending of the curtain has important symbolical meaning. Let us consider the following facts. During the lifetime of Jesus, a definite connection between him and the temple was established by the Synoptic Gospels. For example, as a child he taught in the temple (Luke 2:46). He said that he would destroy the temple and renew it again (John 2:19; Matthew 26:61; 27:40). He announced a new kind of worship in spirit and truth (John 4:24). The Christ was greater than the temple. When he died, the symbolic act of the rending of the temple veil bore witness to him as the one who gives new access to God. The second curtain separated the Holy of Holies from the rest of the temple; no one was permitted to enter the Holy of Holies except the high priest, who entered only once each year to make propitiation for the people. When the curtain was torn, the separation between the presence of God and the people was removed, because the death of Jesus opened the way for everyone and made access to God possible without a human mediator. The tearing of the curtain meant that the Holy of Holies was profaned; everyone could now look into it; its exclusiveness was destroyed. This made it no longer anything holy or mysterious. God had left the temple. The curtain was torn, thus signifying a new way of worship to be based upon the sacrifice of Jesus Christ.

3. *An earthquake.* The earthquake is reported by only one

[4] Josephus, *op. cit.*, book 6, chap. 5, par. 3, pp. 824-825.

Gospel writer, with the following words: ". . . and the earth shook, and the rocks were split" (Matthew 27:51). Whether this was an historical event or not, perhaps no one ever will be able to say with certainty. Earthquakes in Palestine are not uncommon, and there is no reason why there could not have been one on Good Friday. There is no further literary evidence concerning this event, possibly due to the fact that no one deemed it necessary to record an event that was not unusual.

If emphasis is put upon the symbolic meaning, however, we may remember that the Jews considered earthquakes as signs of God's anger; thus, the earthquake would symbolize again the reaction of God toward the execution of Jesus. But this miracle, as indeed all the miracles contemporaneous with the death of Jesus, may symbolize something more. It may point to the fact that the death of Jesus affected the whole universe, including the earth itself, the heavenly bodies, and everything that God created. According to the Genesis account, the ground was cursed as a result of sin. Then, at the death of Jesus, the earth shook and the curse was lifted. The sun was darkened, and the effect of the death of Jesus extended even to the heavenly bodies.

One of the most wonderful teachings of Christian theology is that because sin destroyed the whole perfect creation of God, redemption by Christ is not limited to a section of creation (human beings only) but includes the whole created universe and restores it to its original condition. "For he has made known to us in all wisdom and insight the mystery of his will, according to his purpose which he set forth in Christ as a plan for the fulness of time, to unite all things in him, THINGS IN HEAVEN AND THINGS ON EARTH" (Ephesians 1:9-10).

4. *Partial resurrection.* This miracle also was recorded by Matthew only, with these words: "the tombs also were opened, and many bodies of the saints who had fallen asleep were

raised, and coming out of the tombs after his resurrection they went into the holy city and appeared to many" (Matthew 27:52-53). The report of this miracle is obscure in that it is supposed to have happened at the time of the death of Jesus, accompanying the earthquake and the splitting of the temple veil; yet the resurrected bodies did not come into the city until after Easter. Compared with the specific listing of witnesses in 1 Corinthians 15:4-8, the appearance "to many" is very vague and is difficult to understand in the light of the importance of the matter. The reference to the "saints" is also vague. All these elements taken together suggest symbolism rather than historical reality. But, even if this report of a partial resurrection is a myth, it still expresses a basic reality, which was a part of the faith of the early Christian community. Their faith, of course, was based upon the proclamation of Jesus Christ himself. The basic idea here is that Jesus broke the power of death and that resurrection (which thus far had been only a distant hope) became a reality through his redemption. Christ was the first to be raised from the dead (see the protective addition in Matthew 27:53, "after his resurrection," and also 1 Corinthians 15:23); but at his second coming the general resurrection will take place, "and the dead in Christ will rise first" (1 Thessalonians 4:16). The reference to the "saints" may mean the "dead in Christ," or the saints of the Old Testament, who, according to very early Christian belief, were saved by the retrospective power of the death of Jesus. This symbolism may also be the first expression of what was later formulated in the so-called Apostles' Creed as the article concerning the descent of Jesus into hell, and which in a similar form is to be found in 1 Peter 3:19 and 4:6.

"Then Jesus, crying with a loud voice. . . ."

Καὶ φωνήσας φωνῇ μεγάλῃ ὁ Ἰησοῦς. . . .

In the discussion of the sixth word it was explained that the loud cry which Jesus uttered immediately before his death was not an inarticulate cry but a prayer. This fact is clearly confirmed by the seventh word as recorded by Luke. However, this problem of Jesus' loud cry must be studied again because now we are approaching the physical death of Jesus. It has been suggested many times that the "crying with a loud voice" had something to do with the immediate death of Jesus. These opinions are based on the accounts of Mark (15:37) and Matthew (27:50), who report simply that Jesus cried and expired. The question is made even more difficult in Mark 15:39, for which there are three reading variants:[5]

1. The centurion "saw that he thus breathed his last."
2. The centurion "saw that he thus cried and breathed his last."
3. The centurion "saw him dying with a cry."

Out of these three, the first variant is the oldest and the best attested, but the second and the third were often used to give added significance to the manner of Jesus' death. Both of the latter readings suggest that Jesus spoke out in an audible way at the moment of his death.

There are two interpretations of this matter. The first one examines the death of Jesus from a medical point of view and tries to explain the loud cry. The second considers the loud cry to have been the sign of a divine action by Jesus. Now, as far as the medical explanation of the cry of Jesus is concerned, even modern exegetes sometimes say that in it may be "a possible hint that Jesus' death was due to the failure

[5] See D. Eberhard Nestle, *Novum Testamentum Graece, ad locum* (Stuttgart: Privileg. Wurtt. Bibelanstalt, 1950).

of some vital organ." [6] The question still remains whether or not the failure of a vital organ would really cause a person in mortal agony to utter a painful cry. As a rule, people don't cry in the moment of their death, especially not when actual death is preceded by an extended period of agony, as is the case in crucifixion. It is well known that most victims of this form of execution were unconscious for a long time before death actually occurred. Although Jesus himself was not unconscious when death came, he did go through a three-hour-long agony, probably with considerable loss of blood and exhaustion, which was even more intensified by his scourging a few hours before. Any statement concerning the medical cause of the death of Jesus must necessarily remain a conjecture; yet, it seems to be extremely improbable that a sensation of very great pain made Jesus cry out in the moment of his death.

The second theory, that the cry was the sign of a divine action by Jesus, maintains that with this cry Jesus actually laid down his life by his own volition and thus fulfilled the words recorded in John 10:17-18: ". . . I lay down my life, that I may take it again. No one takes it from me, but I lay it down of my own accord. I have power to lay it down, and I have power to take it again. . . ." Thus, the cry would be a sign of the divine authority of Jesus. S. John Chrysostom in his Homily 88 explained the text this way, and he also added that the centurion believed because Jesus died "with power." [7] Similar views still survive today in assertions that

---

[6] See S. MacLean Gilmour in *The Interpreter's Bible* on Luke 23:46 (New York: Abingdon Press, 1952), vol. 8, p. 412. There are, of course, other scholars who hold a similar view. A fine summary of all contrasting opinions concerning the medical cause of the death of Jesus is in J. Blinzler, *The Trial of Jesus* (Westminster, Md.: The Newman Press, 1959), pp. 258ff.

[7] S. John Chrysostom, *The Nicene and Post Nicene Fathers*, Ser. 1, (New York: The Christian Literature Company, 1888), vol. 10, p. 521.

the loud cry of Jesus was the "shout of a victor," and that this cry was what impressed the centurion; namely, that Jesus died as a triumphant hero.[8] Although such fine speculations may be theologically sound, a systematic view of the passion narratives gives a much simpler explanation. The "loud cry" had neither a physical nor a supernatural cause. It was a prayer that Jesus uttered just before he died.

If there is anything in this account that should provoke thought, it is the fact that up until the moment of his actual death Jesus was able to preserve a clear consciousness and pray in sensible words. Indeed, he may have refused to take the cup which contained the narcotizing drink because he wanted to drink fully the cup that contained the redemptive will of God (Matthew 26:42). This complete obedience of Jesus makes his sacrifice perfect because it is the result of a willing acceptance and a conscious execution of his messianic mission. His consciousness up until the last may be termed miraculous. It would stand to reason that, after the preceding torture and after hanging on the cross for some time, he might have fallen into a state of semiconsciousness or coma. That he did not gives us reason to believe that God himself kept him conscious for the purpose of fulfilling his redemptive plan.

"Father. . . ."

Πάτερ. . . .

This word "Father" is not in the psalm which Jesus quoted. He added it, not deliberately, but naturally, as he always did when referring to, or personally addressing, God in his unique relationship of sonship. Although the significance of the use of this word was explained in the first chapter, it is worth

---

[8] Frederick C. Grant in *The Interpreter's Bible,* on Mark 15:37-39, vol. 7, p. 407.

noting again that the consciousness of this relationship remained alive in Jesus even in the last minutes of his earthly life. There can be no question about God forsaking Jesus, or Jesus acknowledging the failure of his mission, or any similar idea; even in the very minute of his death Jesus declared that the relationship between God and himself is the relationship between Father and Son. He died in this knowledge in perfect peace.

". . . into thy hands I commit my Spirit."

. . . εἰς χεῖράς σου παρατίθεμαι τὸ πνεῦμά μου.

This sentence is taken from Psalm 31:5 which reads in its full form as follows: "Into thy hand I commit my spirit; thou hast redeemed me, O Lord, faithful God." The rabbinic literature refers to this verse in connection with the evening prayer, recommending that the Israelite, before going to sleep, should entrust himself to the mercy of God with this verse.[9] We know that the evening prayer was generally practiced by the Jews in the time of Jesus[10] and that it was a private prayer and not a congregational one. We are safe in assuming, therefore, that when Jesus Christ spoke this sentence he was following a common practice of his day, and probably a personal practice of his own, saying the evening prayer in the words of Psalm 31:5.

But why would Jesus say an evening prayer at three o'clock in the afternoon when sunset was still several hours away? It was because he was near death, and death and sleep were closely associated in the Jewish mind. A common way to express someone's death in the Old Testament was to say that

---

[9] Strack-Billerbeck, *op. cit.*, vol. 2, p. 269.
[10] Stauffer, *op. cit.*, p. 142.

"he slept with his fathers" (Genesis 47:30; 2 Samuel 7:12; 1 Kings 2:10; 1 Kings 11:43) ; and in Daniel 12:2 the dead are described as ". . . those who sleep in the dust of the earth. . . ." Similarly, in the New Testament the word "sleep" may mean death, and the verb "to fall asleep" often means to die *(hupnos* and *koimaomai)*. A well-known text in this respect concerns the death of Lazarus:

> ". . . [Jesus] said to them, 'Our friend Lazarus has fallen asleep, but I go to awake him out of sleep.' The disciples said to him, 'Lord, if he has fallen asleep, he will recover.' Now Jesus had spoken of his death, but they thought that he meant taking rest in sleep. Then Jesus told them plainly, 'Lazarus is dead' " (John 11:11-14) .

The same use is found in Acts 7:60 where the death of Stephen is described with these words: ". . . he fell asleep. And Saul was consenting to his death." For the religious Jew, sleep and death had something in common with each other, just as, on the other hand, to be awake and to live were felt to be similar to each other. When we sleep, we are entirely outside of our own control; we are unconscious of our existence; we are "dead" to the world. It is in the condition of being awake that we realize that we are alive, that we breathe, that the life-giving element in us is at work. Thus, sleep can be rightly conceived of as an "image of death," and death can very well be compared with sleep, as the religious Jews did in the time of Jesus. In the face of immediate death, just before "falling asleep," Jesus Christ said his evening prayer: "Into thy hands I commit my Spirit. . . ." In so doing he followed a generally accepted custom of his religion by offering the traditional prayer.

Within the theology of Luke these words, spoken by Jesus Christ under these special circumstances, have a much deeper meaning than if they were coming from any pious Jew ready to depart this life. Very significant in this connection is the use of the word "spirit." In the Greek text, the word *pneuma* is used, as it is in the corresponding text in the Septuagint. In the Hebrew text of Psalm 31 the word is *ruah*. Both the Greek and the Hebrew words have different meanings, among which the most important are: wind, breath, the divine creative power of God, the life-giving element within man. When the death of Jesus is described in the next sentence of the text, the verb *exepneusen* is used, which is derived from the same basic root as *pneuma* and means "to breathe out." The underlying idea is, of course, that in the moment of death, the life-giving element, the spirit, is breathed out of the physical body, which then returns to dust. Consequently, in the story of the raising of the ruler's daughter, Luke says that "her spirit RETURNED, and she got up at once . . ." (Luke 8:55). There is, therefore, an existence of the spirit which is independent of the body. In later Judaism the notion was quite common that the *pneuma* or *ruah* is essentially the ego of a person. The ego continues to exist after the death of the physical body and can be personally identified. Although the idea of the spirit has a long line of development, and the use of the word itself within the Scriptures is by no means simple, we cannot escape the feeling that the evangelists, in describing the death of Jesus, were pointing to a continued existence of the ego of Jesus Christ after his death. Luke, following Mark, says that Jesus "breathed out" (the spirit), but in Matthew 27:50 a much stronger expression is used, that is, *aphēken* to *pneuma,* which has been translated with "yielded up his spirit." Finally, John says *paredōken to pneuma,* which means that Jesus "gave up" or "handed over the spirit" (John 19:30). The last two expressions (from Matthew and John) may even suggest a voluntary action of Jesus, by which he handed over his spirit to God out of his own will at this particular moment. The spirit of Jesus is, therefore, alive, even after the death of his physical body. It is completely in accordance with this thinking that in the post-resurrection appearances and in later theology the risen Lord is always pictured as the "Pneuma-Christ."

When uttered by a pious Jew retiring for the night, the phrase, "Into thy hands I commit my spirit," may suggest a quiet resignation to the fact that sleep is an image of death, and whoever prepares for sleep should prepare for death. But coming from the lips of Jesus, as the evangelists pictured him, this sentence points not to death, but beyond death to life. It is as if he had said: "I am ready to leave this world, my Father, and I place myself again at your disposal." Jesus did not occupy himself with the idea of death in the sense that death would be the cessation or the absence of life. Even as he faced death on the cross, he was occupied with the idea of life which awaited him. He was looking forward to being "in Paradise" soon, and he even assured the repentant revolutionist of the same prospect. Hence, his last words on the cross were not a preparation for death, but rather a preparation to enter a life in close communion with God the Father. Thus, the passion of Jesus Christ ends not with the victory of death, because even at this point we gain a glimpse of the glory of Easter and the awakening of a new morning. The last words of Jesus from the cross and, indeed, his very death give assurance of the final triumph of life through the faithfulness of God, which is stronger than the power of death and all the evil forces that are yet active in this present age.